Contents

1.	Introduction	
2.	Who are Lay Dominicans?	
3.	This is my Story	
4.	Growing in the Spirit of St Dominic	19
5.	Dominicans at Prayer	26
6.	The Keep, Listen and Ponder the Word	36
7.	Lectio Divina	41
8.	To Praise, To Bless, To Preach	45
9.	Unfolding a Tradition	48
10.	The Dominican Family	54
11.	The Journey - *Formation*	60
	Preparation for admission	61
	Guide and Candidate	61
	Formation after admission	63
13.	The Nine Ways of Prayer of St Dominic	64
14.	Devotion: *Prayer of the Church*	67
	The Rosary	69
	A Prayer of Two Words	71
	The Divine Smile	73
	Truth	74
15.	Short Lives: *St Dominic*	76
	St Catherine	79
	St Martin de Porres	84
	Giorgio Frassati	87
	Jonathan W. Nobles	90
	Agnes McLaren	92
	Honoria Magaen and Honoria Burke	94
16.	A Journey in the Spirit	96
17.	Prayers and Blessings	103
18.	Short Bibliography and Internet Resources	110

Introduction

"Growing in the Spirit of St Dominic" is a guide for Lay Dominicans. Its aim is to foster Dominic's spirit, "being alive in God for others." The foundation stone at Prouille carries the figure of a lamb standing before a Resurrection Cross, an emblem of hope, the symbol of the first preachers. Inspired by Dominic, Lay Dominicans share this hope and share his ministry.

The book suggests ways in which we may grow in this spirit, each generation in its own way, as Catherine, Giorgio Frassati, Agnes McLaren, Jonathan Nobles and others have done in theirs. The section on formation offers, through a weaving of prayer, study and discussion, a planned programme for new members and a way of renewal for all.

It is the work of many hands. A word of thanks: to Mary O'Donovan for editing the text, to Maureen O'Leary, Aidan O'Neill, Deirdre Rooney, Brendan Clifford, Geraldine Flannagan, Marie Ronan, Malachy O'Dwyer, John O'Brien, Raymond O'Donovan and others who through their contributions, encouragement and criticism made it possible.

Simon Roche, OP

Who are Lay Dominicans?

We are lay people who are Dominicans
and members of the Dominican Order.
Our inspiration is St Dominic.
His mission was to preach Jesus Christ
and bring the Gospel message to all
but especially those who felt lost,
confused or had gone astray.

We form one family with the friars and the sisters.

We share
in the apostolic mission of the Order and
actively share in the life of the Church.

We are a mixed bag of saints and sinners, world wide we are over 100,000.

We meet regularly to pray and study together and share each others joys, problems, and hope. We reflect on the Word of God seeking inspiration for our own lives and the lives of others.

If the Dominican project is preaching how does a lay person participate in this mission?

Fr Timothy Radcliffe explains:
"Being a preacher, means that every one of us is sent by God to those whom we meet. A wife is sent to her husband, a husband to his wife. Each is a word of God to each other." The members of the Dominican Chapter in Norfolk prison, Massachusetts are "sent to be a word of hope in a place of suffering... Preaching in a pulpit has always been a small part of our preaching... one could argue that Dominic wished to carry the preaching of the Gospel out of the confines of the Church into the street. He wished to carry the Word of God to where people are living and studying, arguing and relaxing."
We preach in different ways, but each Lay Dominican receives the grace of preaching and exercises that grace in the way they live.
Addressing the Dominican Family in Manila,
Fr Timothy quotes St Paul:

*"You are a letter from Christ...written not with ink
but with the Spirit of the living God, written not on tablets of stone,
but on the tablets of the human heart."*
St Catherine of Siena was a preacher not just in what she said
and wrote, but in giving others strength.
When the Pope lost courage she helped to stiffen his resolve.
"To affirm others with a word or a smile is to preach.
To be present to those who mourn is to preach.
In some situations the most effective word may be silence!
What you are is a preaching."

Dominic: This is My Story

Early Years
I was born in Caleruega in Northern Spain on the frontier between Christianity and Islam. Hot summers, piercing cold winters. All the family was affected by my mother's concern and care for the poor. My elder brother Anthony continued that concern in the house which he opened to offer hospitality to tramps, pilgrims and scholars. Mames, my younger brother joined me in the preaching. After spending my early years at home I went to my uncle, who was parish priest at Gumiel. He shared his love of the psalms and the prayer of the Church.

At fourteen I went to Palencia to study. In the beginning I lived in a hostel, then by myself with my own room and belongings. I enjoyed the study but my mind was already set on being a priest and was impatient to finish my secular studies so that I could begin to study theology at which I spent four years.

Famine was a frequent visitor to the region. When I was studying theology the harvest failed, people streamed into the city in search of food. As food grew short the pleas of the poor knocking on doors was ignored. Food and grain were hoarded. There was fear and guilt as people lay dying in the streets. How could anyone study on dead skins when people were dying of hunger. My books and belongings did not raise much considering the need of the people and so was born the idea of starting a charity. Other students and some of the masters came to help. Much later in Fanjeaux I wrote to some of these friends and they were the first to join me in the preaching after the death of Bishop Diego.

It was while in Palencia that a young woman told me about the plight of her brother who had been taken prisoner by the Moors and was being held for ransom. I offered to help but it was not needed.

While in Palencia, I received an invitation to join the Cathedral Chapter at Osma. Diego was the prior of the community. It became my home after completing my studies for the priesthood and ordination, a life centred on the Eucharist and the Hours of the Office. When appointed sub-prior I was responsible for the preaching and services in the cathedral.

Journey with Bishop Diego
When Diego became bishop he took me on two trips to Northern Europe. On the first we stopped in Toulouse. The owner of our lodging was an Albigensian. I spent the night talking to him and eventually won him to the faith.

In northern Europe we came in contact with peoples who had never been evangelised. This sparked in our hearts a desire to be missionaries. With this

This is My Story

in mind Diego decided to return to Spain via Rome. In Rome he requested Innocent III permission to join the mission in Northern Europe. Gently, the Holy Father refused, bishop Diego should continue as bishop of Osma! A moment of disappointment. I never ceased to hope and plan, that one day, I would become a missionary to the Cumans.

The Albigensians

We began our journey home to Spain travelling through Italy and Southern France where we met Albigensians, good people who had lost their way, drifting away from the church. Instead of believing in one God they believed in two principles, one the author of evil, the other of all that is good. The evil principle was the creator of all matter. Material creation, they taught, was evil. This had wide ranging consequences. Since the body is composed of matter it is evil and since marriage results in the birth of children and more matter, it is evil. Life was a struggle between the evil and good principle. Salvation for the Albigensian, was achieved through liberating the soul from the body. Some of their adherents chose suicide to achieve this. It was a teaching that struck at the root of civilization.

The Day that Changed my Life

In June 1206 we arrived in Montpellier, a day still vivid in my memory. It changed my life. As we entered the walled town we met the Papal Legate and the preachers who were leading the mission to the Albigensians. They were dispirited, their preaching making no impact and they turned to Bishop Diego for advice. After listening to them Diego said: "I do not think that you are setting about this in the right way. In my opinion you will never be able to bring these people back to the faith just by talking to them, because they are much more inclined to be swayed by example… "So what do you advise us to do, they enquired." "Do what you see me doing."

Diego pointed out that the greatest asset the Albigensians possessed was their evangelical quality. If the Papal preachers were to have any credibility they must imitate the life style of the apostles and preach in poverty. It was more than they could stomach so Diego offered to lead them. He sent most of our companions back to Osma with the horses and provisions.

So began the enterprise known as the preaching or the preaching of Jesus Christ. The Montpellier event was to occupy the rest of my life. We abandoned the grand retinue of the Legate and set out on foot two by two in imitation of the apostles. This method we followed for almost two years. The Albigensians launched a counter-offensive of preaching. We met in debate in many of the towns and villages in the area: Pamiers, Montreal, Fanjeaux and Lavaur. On one

Growing in the Spirit of St Dominic

occasion at Fanjeaux a great crowd of believers and unbelievers assembled. My statement of the faith was chosen to defend our position. With the arguments of the opposition it was submitted to three judges who were appointed to judge the debate. There was a long verbal tussle but the judges could not agree on the winner. Eventually they decided that our written documents should be submitted to trial by fire. A big fire was lit and the Albigensian document was consumed by the fire. The one written by myself remained unharmed, "it actually leapt a long way out of the fire... They threw it in again and it seemed to jump out again". Such debates took place throughout the region and attracted much excitement but few conversions.

I often visited the limestone promontory in Fanjeaux to pray. Below the great plain stretched northeast and west to the horizon, and at the foot of the hill was Prouille which had been devastated by war. It was a place to gather my thoughts and to pray over the lands controlled by the Albigensians, that God would grant me true charity that would be effective in winning their salvation. It was while I was there that the inspiration for the monastery below at Prouille was born, in response to the plight of young women seeking to live lives dedicated to God, many with Albigensian backgrounds. Bishop Fulk, the bishop of Toulouse agreed to give the sanctuary at Prouille. It took time to establish. First they lived in the remains of the sanctuary. There were over twelve in the first community in March 1207. On April 17th I received a gift to support the community. I took responsibility for their spiritual needs and William Claret one of my first companions took charge of their material needs. It was a joint community, eventually there would be four friars assigned there. Besides being the monastery of the sisters it was the centre of the preaching.

Lay People Join the Movement – the Death of Bishop Diego
On the 8th August 1207 a group of lay people including married couples offered themselves and their property to the preaching. The year 1207 was full of activity. At the end of the year occurred an event which threw the mission into chaos. Late in 1207, bishop Diego returned to Spain to settle his affairs with the intention of returning. A few days after reaching Osma he fell ill and died on the 30th December 1207. A terrible shock, my bishop and my friend, the inspiration of the preaching was dead.

Three weeks later another disaster occurred. Peter of Castlenau, the Papal Legate, over all in charge of the preaching crusade, was murdered. The effect of these deaths on the preaching was devastating. Dispirited, all the other missionaries left. I was alone.

I decided to stay and continue what Diego and I had begun. The Church reacted in a dramatic way to the murder of the Papal Legate. In June 1209 a military crusade began. In the beginning there was indiscriminate pillaging and it was not until 1212 that peace was established around Fanjeaux and Prouille. The Catholic leader of the crusade was Simon de Montfort. He and his family became firm friends. He generously helped the group at Prouille and myself at Fanjeaux. I baptised his daughter and officiated at the marriage of one of the family.

Fanjeaux
Fanjeaux was my base, this small hill town rising out of the plains, surrounded by Albigensian territory. My home was a stable. Little did I realise that Fanjeaux would be the centre of my work for nearly seven years. In the beginning, preaching and caring for the needs of the community at Prouille occupied my time. With continuous hostilities travel was difficult but I managed to continue preaching from Fanjeaux. In 1209 I was in Carcassonne, in 1210 I spent a lengthy period in Toulouse. During the Lent of 1213, I was back in Carcassonne preaching each day in the cathedral. The following year I returned to Fanjeaux and the bishop appointed me parish priest of the town. Alone after the death of Diego, I wrote to friends in Palencia who had generously helped at the time of the famine and asked if any of them could come and join me. Names that spring to mind are William of Claret, Dominic of Spain, Stephen of Metz, Noel, Vitalis, my lay friends and a few Cistercians formed the nucleus of a new preaching.

On one occasion returning to Fanjeaux I fell into the hands of would-be assassins. Eventually, they sent me on my way. On another occasion praying in the chapel of St Antoine near the Garonne I was able to help in the rescue of forty English pilgrims whose boat overturned in the river. Swollen rivers were always a menace. Many lost their lives including our own Brother Noel, who succeeded me as the prior of Prouille.

Toulouse
Then, suddenly, everything changed. Toulouse was freed from the control of the Albigensians. The Cardinal Legate asked me to transfer the centre of the preaching to Toulouse and at the beginning of 1215, I moved to the town. A time of war, prostitution was rife and with the help of Bishop Fulk who himself had been a wandering troubadour before becoming a Cistercian and then bishop a hospice was opened for my street friends. But there was never enough money, perhaps people felt a little squeamish about the project! Neither my efforts nor those of Bishop Fulk were enough to gain sufficient support. I appealed to Pope Honorius III to write to the city on their behalf. Later the hospice was established as a religious community.

Growing in the Spirit of St Dominic

The Preaching of Jesus Christ
My earlier visits to Toulouse had made me many friends. There was great interest in the Preaching and a number of people expressed the wish to join. In April, 1215, Peter Seila gave three houses to the preaching and I received Peter and a brother Thomas as members of our first community in Toulouse. They were the first professions. This now became the cradle of the preaching of Jesus Christ. The largest house was next to the city wall near the castle and allowed easy exit from the city to the road leading to Fanjeaux and Prouille.

With the departure of the Papal Legate in June, Bishop Fulk formally approved the establishment of our house and assigned the work of preaching to all the members of the community and those who might later join. "I institute as preachers in our diocese Brother Dominic and his companions whose purpose is to acquit themselves as religious, travelling on foot and to preach the Gospel word of truth in evangelical poverty." The community in Peter Seila's house was constituted a preaching and the office of preaching was given to the community. On our preaching journey's we depended on the generosity of the people for our food and shelter and the bishop made provision for the community at Toulouse. He set aside one-sixth of the Diocesan revenues to support the community in books and food. He was truly, a good friend. Our preaching now was to be directed not only to heretics but to believers as well. We made the ten minute walk to the chapel of St Romain each day for Mass and it was in the Chapel that I gave the habit and professed the young John of Navarre.

Study in the Service of Preaching
As our numbers grew the need for a solid formation in preaching became a concern and so, in the Summer of 1215 I took my six companions to the theological lectures of an Englishman, Alexander Stavensby. A good theological formation is an indispensable preparation for preaching. Alexander became a firm friend, and invited the brothers to England when he became a bishop. Others, joined our community including William Raymond and on the 28th of August, John of Spain. Indeed the house was no longer large enough and we spilled over into the other houses to accommodate our growing number.

At the beginning of September, I accompanied Bishop Fulk to the Fourth Latern Council. It was the end of the summer and so the route over the Alps was open. It was an opportunity to meet Pope Innocent III and ask for confirmation of an order which would be called, and would be the Order of Preachers. Over four hundred bishops and eight hundred abbots attended the Council. In the first days of October, the Holy Father, received bishop Fulk and myself. We spoke of the Preaching in Toulouse and we both requested the Holy Father to confirm an Order which would be an Order of preachers. I sought confirmation of the

This is My Story

title and the Preaching. The title had already been granted by Bishop Fulk. What we now sought was confirmation by the Pope. He would not give an immediate reply but referred it to Cardinal Ugolino who would himself be pope. I had a number of meetings with one of his assistants. The problem was Canon 13 of the Council which forbade the formation of new religious Orders. Some days after the 14th of December when the principal work of the Council had been completed we met the Pope again. He confirmed the revenues and gifts which had helped to establish our foundations at Prouille and Toulouse and asked Bishop Fulk to assign us a Church in the city. Then he asked me to return to the brothers in Toulouse and chose some approved rule. When this was done, I was to return to the Pope to receive all that had been asked.

In January 1216 we started for Toulouse, in February we passed through Narbonne. I went straight to Prouille to share the good news with the community and then to Toulouse for the Lenten preaching. After Easter we gathered to celebrate our first chapter where we chose the Rule of St Augustine adopting certain customs surrounding our daily life. Our project was preaching so everything was ordered to facilitate our mission. When bishop Fulk returned from France in June he held a meeting of the Cathedral Chapter and discussed the Pope's request. The diocese generously gave us the Church of St Romain: "to the prior and master of the preachers." In July because of the huge earth works being constructed around the castle next to Peter Seilan's house, we moved to premises adjoining St Romain. We were blessed in our neighbours who gave us extra land. "At this Church of St Romain a cloister was soon built, with cells above it suitable for studying and sleeping in. At that time the brothers numbered sixteen."

Confirmation of the Order

On the 12th of July 1216 Pope Innocent unexpectedly died. Two days later Honorius III was elected. It was with some trepidation that I set out for Rome to seek confirmation of the Order and our choice of the Rule of St Augustine. In Rome I consulted Cardinal Ugolino who assured me that the confirmation asked for and promised by Innocent III would be granted. On my visit to the Curia I was asked to set down in detail the provisions we asked to be incorporated in the Papal Bull of approval. The Pope granted these at an audience and it was approved at a meeting of a consistory of the cardinals. On December 22, at St Peter's we received the documents so long desired. It confirmed the foundation of the Order. It was a moment of great joy. During the next five years the Holy See issued over 60 Bulls and letters in favour of the Order. On the 11th of February 1218, Pope Honorius issued the Letter to the people of Toulouse asking them to support the hospice for my street friends.

Growing in the Spirit of St Dominic

While I was in Rome, news of the deterioration of the situation in Toulouse reached the Pope. The people had rejected Simon de Montfort and Bishop Fulk expressed the wish to resign. Honorius III refused and wrote a touching letter of encouragement.

Mission to the World

Being present at the Latern Council and visiting Rome deepened my awareness of the universality of the Church and its mission. My vision for ourselves was transformed beyond the immediate challenge of the Albigensians. Our mission was the world.

Besides preaching, and visiting those in the towers of the city walls I had time to visit all of Rome. On one occasion, praying in St Peter's, I had a sense of the presence of St Peter and St Paul. One gave me a staff the other a book with the words: "Go and preach, for God has chosen you for this ministry." Then I saw, as it were, the brothers going two by two, preaching throughout the world. At the house of Cardinal Ugolino I met William of Montferrat, a young man who had come on pilgrimage to Rome. We became friends and I confided my own longing to become a missionary in Northern Europe. We decided that William should go to Paris and study theology on the understanding that when I had completed organising the Order we would both go as missionaries to the Cumans.

Dispersal

I returned to Toulouse with a new vision for the future. On the way I visited Prouille and the brothers came to join the community at St Romain where we shared all that had occurred in Rome. Toulouse was engulfed in strife with Simon de Montfort. The city was steadily being isolated from the surrounding countryside. It was a time of decision. Invoking the Holy Spirit, I called the brothers together and told them I had decided to send them away. I did not want everyone to continue living here. The announcement of the dispersal caused amazement. Not everyone was pleased. Bishop Fulk, Simon de Montfort and the Archbishop of Narbonne urged me to reconsider but I felt sure it was the right decision. Four brothers set out for Spain, two of who whom would later go to Bologna. Two groups set out for Paris one led by Matthew of Paris with letters from the Pope to make the Order known there and to establish a house for study and preaching. The second group which included my half brother Mames reached Paris first and rented a house. Later, through the help of Honorius III, we moved to the hospice of St Jacques on the 6th of August 1218. In the same year a group of young brothers went to Orleans. At the beginning of 1218, I sent some brothers to Bologna where they lived in great poverty with barely enough to eat. St Romain was not abandoned, those who came from Toulouse were assigned there. The dispersal was an emotional time, we felt we might never be all together again.

This is My Story

In the middle of September 1217, I set out for Rome. It was one thing to work in a diocese where we were accepted as itinerant preachers quite another elsewhere. There was great uneasiness regarding itinerant preachers! To succeed, we needed the support of the Pope. I passed through Bologna one of the great university cities of the time with over a thousand students and on reaching Rome in February sought a meeting with the Pope. He was most supportive and between 1218 and 1221 he issued a whole series of recommendations introducing us to bishops everywhere. A phrase that constantly turns up in these letters are the words: "With kindness admit the brothers to exercise the office of preacher, to which they have been assigned." One day, two brothers arrived at my lodging from Spain. I sent them to Bologna as the nucleus of that foundation. A little later, brothers Bertrand and John arrived from Paris with news of the community there. There were difficulties everywhere, but difficulties are there to challenge us. Pope Honorius sent a letter to the University of Paris asking the university "to find a suitable lodging for these poor religious in one of the hospices for poor students." It was this letter which brought about the move to St Jacques already mentioned.

I preached throughout Lent in various churches and convents in Rome. A number of young men came forward to join us among them an older vocation, Reginald of Orleans. He was an extraordinarily able man who had taught canon law for five years in Paris. Reginald was a fine preacher and a great catch. He became the superior and inspiration of the community in Bologna.

In May I set out to visit the brothers throughout Europe visiting Bologna, then Prouille, Toulouse and St Romain where the number of brothers had grown, then to Spain which I had left thirteen years before. Vocations began to multiply. Returning to Toulouse I was joined by brother Bertrand for the journey to Paris. About thirty brothers greeted us at St Jacques. Matthew of France had done well. We had been accepted as students in the University. It was now the summer of 1219. Again, following the intervention of Pope Honorius, Master Jean de Barastre began to give lectures in St Jacques. It was on its way to becoming a school of theology. One drawback was that we were not permitted to celebrate Mass or preach in the chapel at St Jacques. We preached in a number of churches in the city and are indebted to the Benedictines who placed one of their churches at our disposal for preaching and hearing confessions. Honorius III wrote and thanked them for this kindness.

It was during this visit that I first met a young theologian Jordan of Saxony. He came to make his confession and we talked at length. Little did I realise that within three years he would succeed me as Master of the Order. In 1219 I had the joy of receiving William of Montferrat. From Paris brothers set out to make the foundation at Orleans and Mames, my brother, returned to Spain and Madrid.

Bologna

In mid July 1219, I left Paris for Italy accompanied by William and Brother John. During the journey we were present when a young boy fell from the terrace of the presbytery at Chatillon-sur-Sain. He was thought to be dead, but revived as we prayed over him. Br. John had great difficulty in crossing the Alps but revived when we reached Italy. A wonderful reception awaited us in Bologna. There was a fine house erected at the Church of St Nicholas and there were a large number of brothers formed by Master Reginald. There was great joy on our arrival. Reginald was a compelling preacher and had won many friends and attracted many vocations. He negotiated with the bishop with the help of Cardinal Ugolino so that we obtained the Church of St Nicholas. The power of his preaching left some nervous lest they be bowled over by his words and find themselves preachers! I was amazed at the growth of the community. Already there were four masters of canon law and philosophy who had joined from the university and many others who had been students. I believed, that as in Paris, the connection with the university would prove a blessing for the future. To have three masters in canon law to help frame the legislation of the Order was a blessing. It was here in Bologna some years later that the custom of singing the Sale Regina began.

I decided that for the future I would make Bologna the centre of my activity, apart from the necessary visits to Rome and preaching in the surrounding dioceses. The poverty we had experienced everywhere at the beginning began to be helped through benefactions and seeing the danger, I felt we should live on alms.

A few days after my arrival I met Diana d' Andalo. She longed to make profession and so she did without their being any convent. I also met many students, visiting them in their lodging, sitting and talking with them in the squares of the city. Some will tell their story elsewhere. I sent some of the brothers to preach in Bergamo where the second house in Italy was established. Others went to Florence where a house was established in November 1219. At Easter in the following year two further houses were established in Verona and Milan.

When we could not fulfil all the requests for preaching I sent novices. Buonvisa went to Piacenza and later described what happened:

> "I was still a novice without any experience of preaching, for I had not yet studied the scriptures. To be dispensed from going I explained my lack of

skill. With very gentle words (Father Dominic) persuaded me that I ought to go; 'Go with assurance, for the Lord will be with you and will put on your lips the words that you should preach.' I obeyed, went to Piacenza, preached there, and God attached so many graces to my preaching that, after having listened to me, three entered the Order of Preachers."

Shortly after he returned to Bologna we set off together for a preaching mission that would last almost ten months. Before leaving I asked Reginald if he would go to Paris where he might make the same contacts he had made at the university in Bologna. He had been a master in Paris for five years and had the necessary gifts to bring understanding between the local clergy and ourselves. There was deep sorrow in the community and in the city at the decision.

St Sixtus and the Nuns
Then, at the end of October, accompanied by Buonvisa I set off to visit the Papal Curia. On the way, we visited Florence where we preached and stayed with our brothers in the home for the poor, St Pancras. We caught up with the Papal Court at Viterbo. On the 11th of November 1219 we met the Pope and reported the progress made in the intervening time. Now we had seven or eight houses and our number was over a hundred. My concern was our freedom to preach. How could we overcome the opposition to our itinerant preaching? Cardinal Ugolino was once again our friend. As he had helped Francis and Clare so he helped us. We obtained a whole series of letters from the Holy Father recommending us across Europe. A few days after the 4th of December the Pope asked me to undertake a mission in Rome - to unite a number of convents of nuns in the city. To assist this process he addressed letters to our communities of brothers and sisters in Fanjeaux, Prouille and Limoux to announce the gift of St Sixtus and to ask their help in this work. Then in the company of the Pope we travelled to Rome and installed ourselves at St Sixtus. In the following six weeks the work of preparing the house for a double community of sisters and brothers began. During these weeks I constantly visited the various groups of the sisters in the city giving talks and allaying their fears about the move to a new home, St Sixtus. Then, I set out for Viterbo to inform Honorius III of progress. On the journey I was plagued with a recurring illness. Years of travel had begun to take its toll. It was on this visit that the Pope gave me the title prior of the Order of Preachers.

The growth in numbers, the experience of living and preaching now suggested that we were ready to formulate constitutions for ourselves. I wrote to the communities in Spain, Provence, France and Italy as well as isolated brothers asking them to choose a number of representatives, (four from Paris) to assemble in Bologna on the 17th of May 1220, the feast of Pentecost for a Chapter of the Order. With great sorrow I learnt of the death of Master Reginald in Paris. The canons forbade his internment in our chapel at St Jacques but the Benedictines offered their church of Notre Dame-des-Champs. Touched by their kindness, I asked the Pope to write and thank them.

The Chapter of 1220

Shortly afterwards, Buonvisa and I set out for Bologna and the Chapter. We stopped in Florence and were joined by the delegates from there. On the eve of the 17th we arrived in Bologna. The house hummed with over thirty delegates from all over Europe, brothers from Madrid and Segovia in Spain, two brothers from Sweden, four from St Jacques including Jordan of Saxony and Matthew of Paris, Paul of Hungary and delegates from Italy. On Pentecost Day we celebrated the Mass of the Holy Spirit and devoted the day to prayer, the next morning I addressed the delegates and we began our first session. At the outset, I asked the brothers to accept my resignation. My failing health and the desire to devote myself exclusively to preaching urged this upon me but they refused. However, we decided that for the duration of the Chapter the definitors, (a small group of brothers) would rule the Order.

In the following days the Chapter discussed and drew up legislation which would form our Constitutions. The Master of the Order and the General Chapter would ensure the unity of the Order for the future. It was decided that there would be a Chapter each year, alternately in Bologna and Paris but that of 1221 would be in Bologna. The chapter took a decision on the mission to Sweden. Further foundations would follow at Amiens, Rheims and Poitiers. At last, the Order was organized, I felt free.

In the meantime, Honorius III had asked me to lead a preaching mission in Lombardy and appointed a number of gifted preachers from different religious orders to join in the mission. In the coming months we travelled throughout Lombardy reaching out to the adherents of the Waldenses and Catharists, good people who had strayed from the Church. I was accompanied by Buonvisa, Ventura and Paul of Venice. For the third time during the year I had a bout of illness in Milan, but soon recovered to return to the preaching. At the end of December I was in Rome.

Three reasons brought me to Rome; to report on the Preaching in Lombardy, to obtain the help of the Curia on some matters concerning the Order, and to finalise the establishment of the nuns at St Sixtus. On my visit to the Curia, I obtained permission to celebrate Mass on a portable table for all our houses. This was a great blessing as we no longer had to go out for Mass to a church or monastery. Numbers in Rome had begun to grow and William of Montferrat had

This is My Story

become a valued member of the papal household. Benedict and Frogier were released for a foundation in Siena.

In the spring of 1221 the Convent of St Sixtus was at last established. On the 21st February the sisters gathered in the Church and all with the exception of one made profession in my hands. After Easter (11th April) another group of sisters joined. At the entrance to the Church I received them into their new home and gave them the white tunic, white scapular and black veil. During the following night a procession led by two cardinals, a number of brothers and myself brought the sisters treasured icon of Our Lady to St Sixtus. In the meantime Bishop Fulk had accompanied sisters from Prouille who would help form the new community which now numbered over sixty. The mission at St Sixtus was complete.

Most of the brothers had to leave St Sixtus as there was no room. I asked the Pope for the church of Santa Sabina and the brothers moved to the Aventine with their books and furniture. Three of four brothers were left in St Sixtus to care for the needs of the sisters. Each evening in May I walked down from Santa Sabina to give the sisters talks, sometimes in the Church, sometimes in the garden by the stream.

One Evening in May
"He came one evening later than usual; accordingly the sisters, thinking that he would not be coming had left their prayer and gone to the dormitory. All of a sudden the brothers rang the small bell which signalled his arrival. All the sisters hurried to the church, the grille was opened, and they found him with the brothers... He then gave them a long instruction and showed himself full of kindness for them. Then he said: 'It would be good to have some refreshment.' Calling brother Roger, the cellarer, he told him to bring some wine and a cup. Dominic asked him to fill the cup to the brim. Then he blessed it and drank it first and after him all the brothers... When they had drunk Dominic said: 'I want all my sisters to drink too. The cup full to the brim... Drink as much as you wish...'"

Around this time, just as Tancred and I arrived at St Sixtus a young man fell from his horse. Thought to be dead, he was brought into a room, and thank God was restored to life.

Once again, for the sixth and last time I left Rome for the north and the preaching in Lombardy. My health was again giving trouble. A few days before the end of May and the Chapter I arrived in Bologna. We were growing by

Growing in the Spirit of St Dominic

leaps and bounds. Over fifty delegates attended the Chapter. Jordan of Saxony was appointed the Provincial of Lombardy and a number of provinces were established; Spain, Provence, Rome… Hyacinth and his brother Ceslaus newly joined were dispatched to Poland and other missions were planned. The longing of Diana d' Andalo to give herself to be a religious continued to be frustrated by her family. In the company of Cardinal Ugolino we managed to visit her.

In June I returned to the preaching in Lombardy. As the summer advanced the preaching drew closer to Bologna. Recurring illness had weakened me. We reached the city in the last days of July where I was struck down by severe bouts of colic and dysentery. At the beginning of August I could no longer remain on my feet.

Recollections of Blessed Jordan

"At Bologna Master Dominic was now approaching the end of his earthly pilgrimage and was seriously ill. He called twelve of the brethren to his sick bed and exhorted them to be eager in their practice of religious life, persevere in the way of holiness… Before his death he told the brothers that he would be more useful to them after his death than he had been during his life."

"With all his energy and with passionate zeal, Brother Dominic set himself to win all the souls he could for Christ. His heart was full of an extraordinary, almost incredible, yearning for the salvation of everyone." (34)

"When the news of the death of the man of God (Bishop Diego) reached the Missionaries who had stayed on in the Toulouse district, they all went back to their homes. Brother Dominic was the only one who carried on preaching the whole time." (31)

"During the night which they spent in lodgings in Toulouse (Dominic) argued powerfully and passionately with their host, who was a heretic and at last brought him back to the faith." (15)

"His face was always radiant with a cheerfulness which revealed the good conscience he bore within him… By his cheerfulness he easily won the love of everybody. Without difficulty he found his way into people's hearts as soon as they saw him." (103-104)

"During the daytime nobody was more sociable and happy with his brothers and companions, but at night nobody was more thoroughly dedicated to keeping vigil and to prayer." (104-105)

Simon Roche OP

Growing in the Spirit of St Dominic

A Lay Dominican is called to be the visible presence of Dominic in the world of today. The most important gift that a founder transmits is a share in his spirit, that particular charismatic manifestation of the Holy Spirit that distinguishes the founder himself. Just as the spirit of Moses was shared among the seventy elders and as Elisha asked Elijah for a double share in his spirit, Dominicans ask Dominic for a share in his spirit.

That spirit is not something easily caught from a book. Rather it is something that is caught from someone, and for Dominicans that someone is Dominic, himself or those imbued with his spirit. Indeed, we may need to catch it more than once because we tend to lose touch. The Constitutions emphasize the importance of Dominic as the model of Dominican life.

The mystery of the communication of the spirit of Dominic within the Dominican Family is a special realization of the mystery of the communication of the Spirit of Jesus in the Church. In the community of the Church we find Jesus. Dominicans find the Spirit of Jesus mediated to us through Dominic.

Jordan of Saxony ends his life of Dominic by urging his followers to walk in the footsteps of St Dominic and to "give thanks to the Redeemer who has given us such a leader." A thorough familiarity with Dominic's spiritual and apostolic character is crucial. Modern scholarship enables us to examine, perhaps better than ever before, the man Dominic. He was a man of immense charm, with great breadth of vision, compassionate to an extraordinary degree, with an incredible zeal for souls, in deep union with God, an organizational genius. Having read a brief outline of Dominic's life let us reflect on certain aspects of Dominic's spiritual and apostolic character with special reference to today.

A Tranquil and Joyous Spirit
With a certain humour, Simon Tugwell has said of him: "Contrary to the previous tradition of religious life, Dominic believed in the virtue of laughter." Jordan of Saxony who received the habit from Dominic and succeeded him as Master of the Order recalls: "No one more than he mingled in the company of his brothers or companions on the road and no one was happier than he."

> "His mind was always steady and calm, except when he was stirred by a feeling of compassion and mercy; and since a happy heart makes for a cheerful face, the tranquil composure of the inner man was revealed outwardly by the kindness and cheerfulness of his expression. He never allowed himself to become angry... his face was always radiant with

cheerfulness... By his cheerfulness he easily won the love of everybody. Without difficulty he found his way into people's hearts as soon as they saw him."

He was always calm and joyful, "full of mercy and friendliness." He cultivated cheerfulness. If he wept, he also knew how to laugh. "Dominic was one of a new type of saints. They appeared first at the time of the spiritual renewal which had taken place towards the end of the eleventh century. Joyousness of heart, outwardly expressed in overflowing goodness and a joyous countenance, was felt to be a gospel characteristic."

Jordan of Saxony had a similar gift for encouraging those who were troubled by "his cheerful presence." Gentle, witty and humorous he had a sense of the funny. When one of his companions reprimanded a group of novices who broke into laughter during night prayer Jordan told them "laugh to your hearts content and don't stop on that man's account."

Dominican spirituality is a joyous spirituality that affirms the goodness of created things and "faith in the absolute priority of God's grace in any human activity..." and so there is no "cramped self concern but trust in God" whom we can trust more than ourselves. A trust that is based on the conviction that we belong to God and that everything that happens to us is a part of God's providence for us and through us for others. Failure or adversity should not diminish inner peace. Such was the tranquil, joyous spirit Dominic transmitted.

Spontaneity
Another trait transmitted by Dominic is spontaneity. The "evidence of the witnesses at the process of his canonization has preserved the sudden spontaneity of his traits and his quick vivid phrases. It is significant that they have been echoed, often unconsciously among his followers for seven hundred years... Spontaneity was to remain a note of Dominican spirituality and perhaps the primary characteristic of its school of prayer."

Spontaneity was evident in the whole of Dominic's life. Many noted that his immediate response to opposition and adversity was joy. Paul of Venice tells us that frequently on the road he would turn to his companion and say: "Go on ahead, let us think of the Saviour." His spontaneous response to meeting the Albigensian inn-keeper was to spend the night talking with him. On the road, when he heard the bell of a monastery or church he immediately changed direction to join the community in prayer. When requests for preaching could not be met by priests he sent a novice: "Go confidently for the Lord will be with you and he will put words in your mouth." When a woman asked him to visit her sick daughter his immediate reply was: "Go home I will pray for her." The next day her daughter was better. When there was a shortage of bread or wine and Dominic was told about it he would answer: "Go and pray, the Lord will provide."

He expected the same spontaneity in others. Stephen of Spain recalled an evening when Dominic sent for him. Like many university students at Bologna, he had gone to hear him preach and had made his confession. "It seemed that Dominic really loved me. Then one night while I and my companions were about to eat supper at our lodgings, Dominic sent one of the brothers to me. He said: 'Brother Dominic says that you must come to him immediately.' I replied: 'I will come when I have eaten. 'No', he said, 'You must come right now.' When he reached the church of St Nicholas Dominic who was waiting for him. He turned to a brother and said: 'Show him how to make the venia.'" Then Stephen placed his hands in those of Dominic and he clothed him in the habit. Stephen said that the whole incident was a source of great wonder to him. He had never said that he wanted to enter religious life!

The Nine Ways of Prayer, reveal another aspect of this spontaneity. It describes the way in which Dominic employed gestures, raised his hands, bowed, stood on tiptoe engaging the whole body in prayer. He felt free to express himself in whatever way he wished. Freedom and spontaneity are interconnected. Those who are free can express themselves in a spontaneous way. If spontaneity was a trait of his Spanish character, it had spiritual roots. It was rooted in a sensitive listening to the Spirit. The great source of his freedom and spontaneity was his intuition of the inspiration of the Spirit. It was the same sensitivity that guided him in the dispersal of the first Brothers from Toulouse. Bishop Fulk, Simon de Montfort and the Archbishop of Narbonne advised him against it, but Dominic politely ignored their advice: "Do not oppose me, I know very well what I am doing."

Then there was his respect for the uniqueness of each person, and so the Dominican spirit has always been marked by individual variety. The saints and the blessed of the Order have achieved sanctity in very different settings: in the studia, in sisters' monasteries and convents, in parish houses, as missionaries, as lay Dominicans or in the itinerant life of the preacher.

The Personal Following of Christ - A Jesus Spirituality
A third characteristic is "Dominic's utter concentration upon the personal following of Christ that was to dwarf all other devotions in the Order," the desire to spend himself for others as Christ had spent Himself on the Cross. That same desire was to drive the greatest missionaries among us across the boundaries of the known world east to Central Asia and later west across the Atlantic and south into the Asia Pacific region.

Growing in the Spirit of St Dominic

Dominic gave the Order its "Jesus Spirituality" its devotion to the humanity of Christ that has so characterized the lives of men and women like Albert, Margaret of Hungary, Thomas, Catherine, Eckhart, Tauler, Rose, Giorgio Frassati and so many others. Inseparable from this devotion to the person of Jesus is devotion to Mary.

An Openness to New Ideas and Charisms
A further characteristic was his openness to new charisms, to new ideas, to truth from whatever source it came. Dominic lived during a time of great social change when the very structures of society were being scrutinized and questioned. He read the signs of his time and committed himself to the future and so his spirit is characterized by an openness to new ideas and charisms required by the changing structures of the time. Furthermore, he saw the need for structures that did not close doors. With his practical genius for organization he made a commitment to structures that were both democratic and flexible, adapted to new and emerging charisms. As if to say, "If there is need for change today, let us remain open to possible change tomorrow." He conceived of the Constitutions not as static pieces of legislation but ones which must be constantly tested and reappraised. Openness to new ideas and charisms, to truth from whatever source it comes whether from the Church, or the secular world continues to challenge us.

This openness to changing needs so characteristic of Dominic also characterized his followers. By way of illustrating this Schillebeeckx cites the example, that though the Constitutions of 1223 1231 stated: "Our brothers may not study the books of pagan writers... and far less may they study the secular sciences." Twenty years later "Albert the Great and Thomas Aquinas were to regard the study of secular sciences and the 'pagan philosophers' as a necessary condition of the preparation and formation of an appropriate Dominican apostolate." Subsequently they were vindicated in this new orientation and the early prohibition was removed from the Constitutions. It is typical of Dominicans down through the ages to have the gift of reshaping the old and combining it with the dynamism of the new. Dominic had this gift.

History indicates that we have not always been faithful to new and emerging charisms and ideas. Ignatius of Loyola was imprisoned in the cellar of one of our Dominican houses. Although Tommaso Campanella wrote in defence of Galileo there were other Dominicans who had a hand in his condemnation. There are many such stories of occasions when we failed to be faithful to our charism, times when as Schillebeeckx says: "Dominicans were no longer Dominicans" because in holding on to old ways of thinking they failed to see the Spirit at work in the new. Dominic on the other hand while cherishing what was good

Growing in the Spirit of St Dominic

in traditional values, saw clearly the needs and possibilities of his own time and situation. Constantly present to God he was present also to the world about him and out of his burning concern for both was born the Dominican Order. "To be present to God" and "to be present to the world" are the qualities that characterized the Dominican spirit throughout its history. In the 19th. century, Henri Lacordaire captured this ideal: "It is the grace of understanding the present century."

Two Key Moments in Dominic's Life
There are two special events or experiences which shaped the story of Dominic's life. The first was his contact with the people of Northern Europe which sparked the desire to be a missionary. We know that from 1206 at the latest Dominic was filled with this desire, a desire that was never fulfilled but one that never died. In 1217 he confided his intention of going to preach in Northern Europe to William of Montferrat: they planned to go together when he had finished organizing the Order. With this in mind he began to grow his beard. Dominic never made it, but when the Chapter of 1221 decided to send a group led by Paul of Hungary to preach the Gospel outside the confines of Christendom the brothers asked to go to the Cumans. They fulfilled Dominic's dream.

The second moment is the Montpellier event. One morning or evening in June 1206, Diego and Dominic entered the walled town where they met and talked with the dispirited papal legates preaching among the Albigensians. Far from consoling them Diego shocked them with a proposal which to them smacked of novelty. Diego and Dominic saw that "the greatest asset that the heretics possessed was their evangelical quality." If the preachers were to have any credibility among the people they too must imitate the life pattern of the apostles, preaching on foot in poverty. It was more than the legates could immediately stomach. They suggested that Diego might lead them and he and Dominic chose to do so. In 1207 Diego returned to Spain leaving Dominic to carry on and so the enterprise known simply as "the Preaching" or "the Preaching of Jesus Christ" began. At its head was the Master of Preaching.

The great weakness of "the Preaching" was the fact that the first participants were religious, chiefly Cistercians, with other commitments. Most stayed on the job for only a few months and Diego died before the problem could be solved. But Dominic continued to play upon the original inspiration. The Montpellier event was to occupy the rest of his life.

The Leaven of Failure
If legend suggests that his early preaching was successful the facts speak otherwise. Vicaire says the most painful trial and contradiction Dominic

Growing in the Spirit of St Dominic

experienced in Southern France between 1204-14 was the "fewness and poor quality of the conversions which were sometimes the outcome of fear." Dominic experienced failure in his preaching; he knew also the loneliness and pain of being abandoned by his fellow workers. Jordan tells us that after the death of Bishop Diego in December "the missionaries… all went back to their homes. Brother Dominic was the only one who carried on preaching the whole time." A time of loneliness and rejection! "Neither his poverty, his extreme austerity… his eloquent preaching, his debates, his miracles, his humility, not all of these together had much effect in converting the Albigensians. The most sober historical conclusion is that Dominic began his preaching career in failure."

If Dominic knew the taste of failure, he remained faithful to his initial inspiration. He worked on in the conviction that in the Lord's time the tide would turn. With Diego he had "founded a true Gospel way, a way of living poorly, praying and preaching Jesus Christ. One day that preaching would be heard." Hope endured in spite of failure. Fidelity in the midst of failure is not the least of Dominic's legacies.

It was not until 1215 that the dream finally began to come true. To safeguard the continuity of "the preaching," the Order was born. Dominic was able to gather a small group of men who were fired by his ideal of preaching the Gospel. Of Dominic and these first companions Bishop Fulk said: "they have committed themselves to travelling religiously on foot, in evangelical poverty, and to preaching the word of evangelical truth."

The project was preaching. He preached to everyone, everywhere. In the beginning, the need was so great that he sent out uneducated men; even novices were not exempt. When a novice, Buonvisa, expressed fear on being sent to preach, Dominic simply told him to go and that he would pray for him.

Study in the Service of Preaching

If, in the beginning, some went out to preach with little preparation, that was not Dominic's intention for the future. He saw study as an integral part of a training programme for the preacher. John of Spain tells us that Dominic always carried with him the Gospel of Matthew and the Letters of Paul and constantly encouraged the brethren to study the New and Old Testaments. In the summer of 1215 Dominic began taking his first companions to the theology lectures of Alexander Stavensby. Two years later in 1217, he asked for and received a letter from the Holy See, a Letter to the University of Paris, commanding that a certain number of theologians be sent to lecture and preach at Toulouse. Dominic never used this letter because the situation at Toulouse deteriorated; instead he sent the brothers to Paris.

This request emphasizes the importance he attached to study and the resolution with which he pursued it. He had no hesitation in enlisting the help of the

Growing in the Spirit of St Dominic

Holy See in promoting his vision. The source of help was unimportant. What mattered was that the teachers possessed the truth and were competent. In a word Dominic wanted excellence. If others excel in one field or another, listen to them, learn from them.

Apostolic Freedom
Finally, a word about apostolic freedom. Cardinal Villot in a letter to the Order in 1970 described Dominic as "stupefyingly free".

For Dominic, freedom of spirit was not an accident but a deliberate choice, an apostolic tool. His itinerant life style, the insistence on mobility, a democratic system of government, the supremacy of the General Chapter in the Order, the submission of his opinions to others, the law of dispensation, a simplified liturgy, the simplicity of Dominican buildings, his openness to new ideas and new charisms, are all aspects of his conviction of the need of apostolic freedom. His very spontaneity was a fruit of this apostolic freedom which he wished to inculcate in his followers, the freedom to preach.

There is nothing that frightens us more than freedom and the responsibility it imposes but for Dominicans, as for others, it is not a matter of choice. It is an essential ingredient of the Dominican Spirit.

We have not always been faithful to it. The pursuit of security sometimes leads us to mortgage our apostolic freedom to institutions and work that offers a certain level of comfort and financial security. This robs us of much more than our mobility. Fearful of losing our security we sometimes see new charisms and new ideas as a threat and thus spontaneity is deadened. Slowly we lose the ability to be creative and make a creative response to the "signs of our times". We are no longer capable of creating a typical Dominican strategy for our day, and are in danger of becoming irrelevant. "Some of our houses" said Vincent de Couesnongle, "are inhabited by Benedictines rather than Dominicans."

Conclusion
A joyous tranquil spirit, spontaneity, the personal following of Christ with all that this entails, an openness to new ideas and charisms, study in the service of the Gospel, an ability to read the signs of the times and a carefully guarded apostolic freedom that enabled him to respond to the challenges of his day characterized Dominic's spirit, and should characterize the Dominican spirit today.

Simon Roche OP

Dominicans at Prayer

"The most powerful prayer, and almost the strongest of all to obtain everything, and the most honourable of all works, is that which proceeds from an empty spirit. The emptier the spirit, the more is prayer and the work mighty, worthy, profitable, praise worthy and perfect. The empty spirit can do everything".

Meister Eckhart

"In whatever way you find God most and you are most aware of God, that is the way you should follow. But if another way presents itself, quite contrary to the first, and if, having abandoned the first way, you find God as much in the new as in the one you left, then that is right".

Meister Eckhart

Dominicans at Prayer

In what he refers to as his definitive study of St Dominic, M. H. Vicaire draws our attention to a portrait by Giovanni Bellini in the National Gallery in London. It is "a moving portrait of the contemplative, with his penetrating gaze turned towards infinity." He asks:

> "Is it really an appropriate image for this efficient founder, indefatigable traveller, missionary, preacher, leader of men and women, for the head and model of the Friars Preachers? And yet this was the image most readily perceived by those who lived with Dominic, the one which former canons at Osma later become Preachers passed on to Jordan of Saxony... It is this image that so overwhelmed the prior of the canons of Castres when he saw Dominic in ecstasy before the relics of St Vincent Martyr that he decided to become a preacher himself. It is the image evoked by the abbot of the canons of St Paul of Narbonne, who speaks of Dominic's whole nights spent in prayer with piercing cries from time to time, 'O Lord, be merciful to your people. What will become of sinners?'"

How did his early companions remember Dominic at prayer? John of Spain, received the habit from Dominic in August 1216. A critic and a rebel he was incensed at Dominic's decision to disperse the brothers and not shy about saying so. When he was assigned to Paris he stubbornly refused to go unless Dominic gave him money for the journey and won his point. Assigned to study in Paris he was on the road again within six months accompanying Matthew of Paris to visit Dominic in Rome. When Dominic's cause was opened in Bologna he was the senior most of the Brothers to give evidence and spoke movingly of the time spent in Dominic's company as he lived and travelled with him through different countries. Of his prayer he said:

> "He prayed more persistently than all the other brothers... He rarely spoke except about God or with God in prayer and he encouraged the brothers to do likewise. He was happy when he was with other people, but in prayer he sobbed and wept."

Rudolf of Faenza adds:
> "Dominic nearly always spent the night in church, praying and weeping there as I saw by the light of the lamp which is in the church, and sometimes I saw him standing on tiptoe with his hands stretched up. Because of the intimacy I had with him I sometimes went and prayed beside him, and I saw in him a fervour in prayer such as I have never seen the like of."

Growing in the Spirit of St Dominic

Stephen, the Provincial of Lombardy confirmed this.

"After Compline, when the common prayer was finished he made the brothers go to the dormitory, while he remained in the Church to pray. And while he prayed, he used to reach such a pitch of groaning and lamenting that the brethren who were near by were woken up by it. He often spent the whole night in the church."

He also repeats the fact that it was Dominic's custom:

"to speak always either of God or with God, whether he was in or outside the house or on a journey. He strongly urged the brothers to act similarly and had the practice inserted into his constitutions... Dominic was more persevering in prayer than any other man I have ever seen."

Stephen also recalled the devotion with which Dominic celebrated Mass:

"I always noticed that his eyes and cheeks were wet with tears during the Canon. It was quite easy for those present to see his devotion and his great fervour during Mass and the way he said the Our Father. I never remember having seen him say Mass with dry eyes."

Jordan of Saxony says he had a special prayer which he often made "that God would grant him true charity which would be effective in winning salvation" for others. He was extremely flexible concerning the place for prayer. He prayed on the road, in parish churches and in monasteries. If there was a special time it was the night.

Details of Jordan's own prayer are recorded in the *Lives of the Brethren* and pattern those of Dominic. The period after Compline and the Office of Readings was reserved for prayer no matter how tired or long a journey had been completed. On such occasions he would spend as much time in prayer as someone could easily walk eight miles! As he walked across Europe it was his unvarying custom to busy himself in prayer and contemplation and taught his companions a simple form of meditation. As they walked along he urged them to choose some mystery, meditate upon it and then share their insights with the others. He frequently walked about a stone's throw ahead singing the *Salve Regina* or *Jesu nostra redemptio* and like Dominic often strayed from his companions who then had to go in search of him. On several occasions he taught young religious how to pray. He taught a novice whom he caught spying on him one night a way of praying to Our Lady and a student who questioned him about the best way to pray was advised to choose those topics which inspire devotion and move the heart.

Personal Prayer, the Dominican Tradition
It is clear that personal prayer occupied an important place in the lives of

both brothers and sisters. Dominic continued the custom borrowed from the monastic tradition of spending two periods in personal prayer, one after Compline, the other after the Office of Readings. Though there is no reference to these in the early Constitutions they are well documented in early Dominican Sources. They are called Orationes Secretae (Secret Prayers). The *Lives of the Brethren* (1256) gives an insight into how the brothers used this time.

> "After Compline as though on pilgrimage they visited all the altars in turn, humbly prostrating before each... This done they did not immediately run back to their studies but in the Church or Chapter room or retiring to corners of the cloisters, they examined their consciences..."

Humbert of Romans gives more detailed information. In his *De Officiis Ordinis* he devotes two sections to the instruction of novices: *Circa Orationem (Prayer)* and *Circa Meditationes (Meditation)*.

In the first Humbert says the novice is not only to be instructed in the psalms and the way in which to pray but also be guided in what to pray about: forgiveness of sin, growth in grace and virtue, in times of perplexity and doubt, in temptation and difficulty, before beginning a new work... But he should not pray for himself alone. He must also be encouraged to pray for his parents, friends and family, for sinners and those who persecute, for those who are ignorant about God and those who are separated from God. Novices are to be encouraged to occupy their free time in such prayer. Humbert also suggests that it is important to choose a suitable place for prayer.

Moving on to the practice of meditation he says that the novice should be instructed to spend some time in meditation and to use those occasions when they are travelling, in the cloister, or when engaged in secret prayer in this way. He also proposes a series of topics: God's gifts, the ingratitude of the human race, creation, redemption, the passion, heaven and hell, the example of the saints... God's mercy and justice. Such subjects when meditated upon will give rise to diverse feelings which in turn will help to arouse a variety of dispositions: hope, sorrow...

Elsewhere in the same work Humbert notes that while the *Office* consists largely of the prayer of praise, secret prayers are more inclined to be prayers of petition. In his reference to personal prayer Humbert suggests the time should not be too long or too short. If too long, the brothers will become over tired and give up the practice, if too short it may tend to suffocate devotion. It suffices, he says, to spend as much time as it would take to say the seven penitential psalms and the litany.

Growing in the Spirit of St Dominic

Spontaneity

Two characteristics which mark Dominican prayer are spontaneity and simplicity. Writing in *Blackfriars* Gervase Mathew, the English Dominican historian says spontaneity is "a note of Dominican spirituality and perhaps the primary characteristic of its school of prayer."

The Nine Ways of Prayer give a vivid description of Dominic's spontaneity and his use of the body in prayer. He felt free to express himself in whatever way he wished. But there was one aspect of his prayer which was more than a distraction to others. He was noisy. Others may have begun to imitate him, for the *Primitive Constitutions* instruct the novice master: "He should teach them... how and what they are to pray and how quietly they should pray, so that they do not disturb others with their roaring." It was Dominic who wrote the section on the office of the Master of Novices, with a twinkle in his eye!

His use of the body in prayer is reflected also in his prayers for others. Raymond Major recounts how Dominic put his hands on him: "I was healed of fever" and Raymond Gerard recalled how he "placed hands on the eyes of a blind man who instantly regained his sight" examples of spontaneous charismatic prayer. After the Office or a meal:

> "he would quickly go and sit down in a place by himself in a room or somewhere, to read or pray, recollecting himself... in the presence of God. He would sit there quietly and open some book... letting... what he had read touch his mind, as if he actually heard the Lord speaking to him... It was as if he were discussing something with a friend: at times he would seem to be racing on impatiently in his mind and in his words; at other times, he would listen quietly and discuss and argue, and then laugh and weep all at once, and fix his gaze and bow his head, speaking quietly again and beating his breast."

The great source of his freedom and spontaneity was his intuition of the inspiration of the Holy Spirit.

Simplicity

A second trait of Dominican prayer is simplicity. Dominic's recorded prayers are direct and simple. Though he spent long periods in prayer, the prayers themselves are short. "O Lord, be merciful to your people, what will become of sinners?" Another aspect of this simplicity is that there is, with a few exceptions, no elaborate methodology. Simon Tugwell in an article *A Dominican Theology of Prayer* suggests that it is typical of Dominican teaching on prayer "that Dominicans do not, very often, make as much fuss about prayer as some other people seem to do. They do not appear to regard prayer as being as difficult or even as important as it is supposed to be in other schemes."

To illustrate this he quotes Bede Jarrett:

> Prayer is too often robbed of all its effects, is reduced to hard and fast rules, is mapped out and labelled and regimented till it hardly seems at all to be the language of the heart. It becomes instead (and the elaborate instruction of so many books on mental prayer simply bear out this view) a highly artificial science, where notices meet us at every step, burly policemen in the guise of theologians bar our passage and definite and well ordered paths, macadamized and straight and uninteresting, stretch out in military fashion to the skyline. All adventure has gone, all the personal touches, and all the contemplation. ... The whole doctrine of prayer from its practical standpoint can be summed up by saying that it is talking to God as a friend talks with a friend... Now this talking as with a friend... involves a view of prayer that should make it very much more easy for me."

An even more striking recommendation is that from a book published for Dominican novice masters in 1951 *Le Pere Maitre* by E. A. Langlais:

> "A direct and active way of praying is the true method: throw yourself into it with all that you are, body and soul, and give of your best... In order to pray, there is no need for us to look for some classic, scientific, artificial method. Prayer is a spontaneous, intimate conversation with God in ourselves... God is not subject to techniques".

It is not introspective soul tinkering. Simplicity also extends to the terminology employed in prayer. For Dominicans meditation is thinking about God. When we use the term mental prayer it is used in contrast to vocal prayer. The only difference is that vocal prayer is prayer said out loud, and mental prayer is not said out loud.

> "It is also a very characteristic Dominican belief that prayer is not the primary criterion of spirituality... It is charity which is all important... A life which has no room for down to earth acts of charity is defective..."

Prayer of Petition
The prayer which characterized Dominic's life was the prayer of petition. When Thomas Aquinas takes up the question of prayer in the Summa, it is a study of the prayer of petition. In a sense, it contains all prayer. Vincent McNabb goes so far as to claim that the prayer of petition "is the absolutely essential prayer,

without which all other prayers would be almost blasphemous."
A young student curious to know what Dominic was up to down in the church during the night stole down and stood behind a pillar and watched him. He heard him cry: "Lord have mercy on your people, what will become of sinners." How many others heard the same prayer? The prayer of petition is in a special way the prayer of an apostle and an area of apostolic collaboration between sisters, brothers and lay Dominicans. In fifty letters written between 1222 and 1236 Jordan of Saxony requested the prayers of Diana and the nuns seventy seven times. He asks Diana to join her prayers to those of the brothers for the salvation of souls assuring her: "by your prayers you will be sharers in the work."

In a letter on the Common Life, Damian Byrne wrote to the Order:

> "Besides communal prayer each one of us needs the space to create that inner silence and aloneness to be with the Lord, to enable us to say for an extended period each day: 'I want to be with you'. Frequently, Dominic would turn to his companion on the road and say: 'Go on ahead let us think of the Saviour' and then fall behind to be alone. We must find a similar space for ourselves..."

The Dominican approach to prayer is very simple, very ordinary. It is not highly organized. There is a freedom which allows of spontaneity. For each one has his or her own touch on God and God touches each one in a singular way. Respect for the uniqueness of each person demands the freedom to discover this.

Liturgical Prayer
In the Monastery of the Holy Rosary on Monte Mario in Rome is a breviary which according to tradition was used by St Dominic. Jordan of Saxony gave this pocket sized breviary to Diana d'Andalo as a souvenir of Dominic on the 8th November 1222.

Is the Monte Mario breviary Dominic's? Internal evidence, in particular some of the antiphons of Advent, suggests it originated in Silos or Osma in Spain or in the South of France between 1200-1230. It is the work of different hands. One of these hands copied the first line of a series of hymns on to a blank page. Fr Leonard Boyle wonders: "Could this possibly be the hand of Dominic?"

The breviary indicates an early adaptation of the Prayer of the Church to the needs of the Preachers. Dominic's experience as a member of the Cathedral Chapter of Osma placed him in the prayer tradition of the canons of the twelfth century. He cherished the Prayer of the Church and even though an itinerant, sought every opportunity to pray with the local church through which he journeyed.

Dominicans at Prayer

Besides the adaptations noted in the breviary, the Primitive Constitutions (1228) indicate an effort to adapt monastic prayer to the life of the Preachers. The Office of Readings and Morning Prayer were said as one hour. Humbert of Romans (1254 63) felt it necessary to defend this innovation so at odds with the earlier monastic tradition. Another innovation was the direction to say the office briskly, in the interests not only of devotion but also of study. This instruction probably dates from 1220. Finally, the practice that each side of choir stand or sit for every alternate psalm was introduced.

It would have been in keeping with Dominic's spirit of adaptability to have suggested to the brothers on their dispersal from Toulouse in 1217 that they should adapt themselves to local customs and pray with the local church. What is clear is that a variety of liturgical practice began to appear.

The General Chapter of 1233 recommends that novices who have money should buy breviaries. The monk with his vow of stability did not need a personal breviary, the itinerant did. The Chapter of 1245 set out to unify Dominican liturgical prayer. This was completed in 1256 when a prototype was approved. Humbert of Romans wrote: "From the beginning there was much diversity in the office. Hence, there was compiled one office for the sake of having uniformity everywhere."

The Prototype is in Santa Sabina. A beautiful book, of extraordinary workmanship, it retains the brilliant colours and clarity of the original scribes as though it had been produced yesterday. It is 750 years old. This is the origin of the Dominican Rite, which was a response to the needs of an international Order confronted by a multiplicity of local liturgies. A monastery might develop its own liturgical practice, a local church have its own liturgy, but an international itinerant group of religious needed a common liturgy so that they could celebrate it wherever they were. As greater uniformity spread in the Church the need for a distinctive Dominican liturgy began to decline.

With minor changes the Dominican Rite continued down to 1923 when the Order adopted the Psalter of Pius X and, in 1969, the Missal and calendar of Paul VI and the new Liturgy of the hours. With the uniformity of the Church's liturgy the need for a distinctive Dominican Rite ended. "Each instance illustrates how the Order prays with the Church, for as the Church changed the arrangement of her Psalter, so did Dominicans and as the church restructured her pattern of prayer, so also did the Order."

Dominic and his Dream
Dominic's purpose was to create an Order of contemplative apostles. Personal and liturgical prayer were indispensable conditions for such an Order. The Mass

is at the centre of each day's prayer and the hours aim at sanctifying each part of the day. In his own life Dominic demonstrated that it was possible to be both a contemplative and an active apostle. Though continually on the move for weeks at a time, he celebrated Mass each day he was near a church. Daily Mass was not widespread in the 13th century and was especially remarkable in the lives of itinerant preachers. Dominic passed this custom to his companions.

The Word Pondered

Letter To Diana
France,
Christmas 1229

I cannot find the time to write you the long letter your love would wish for and I would so gladly send; none the less I do write, I send you a very little word, the Word made little in the crib, the Word who was made flesh for us, the Word of salvation and grace, of sweetness and glory, the Word who is good and gentle, Jesus Christ, and him crucified, Christ raised up on the Cross, raised in praise to the Father's right hand: to whom and in whom do you raise up your soul and find there your rest unending for ever and ever. Read over this Word in your heart, turn it over in your mind, let it be sweet as honey on your lips; ponder it, dwell on it, that it may dwell with you and in you for ever. There is another word that I send you, small and brief; my love, which will speak for me to your love in your heart and will content it. May this word too be yours, and likewise dwell with you for ever.

Farewell, and pray for me.

Jordan

To Listen, Keep, and Ponder the Word

A Man of the Book
Hidden in an alcove, facing the door to the original convent at Santa Sabina, is a large statue of St Dominic. It is the image of a man with a strong compassionate face, striding towards some unseen destination. He carries his walking stick and a book. The earliest pictures of Dominic invariably represent him carrying a book.

John of Spain records: "Both by word and letter" Dominic "urged the brothers of the Order to make a constant study of the Old and New Testaments. I heard him say this and saw the letters. He always carried Matthew's Gospel and Paul's letters with him. From studying them so much he almost knew them from memory." Fra Angelico pictures Dominic with a book, often he is sitting and pondering the word of scripture. The *Nine Ways of Prayer* picture Dominic hurrying off after meals or choir to find a place to sit quietly, to read and pray.

The Word read and pondered is the great source of our preaching as it was of Dominic's. The "Word of God is alive, it is life" and Jesus gave instructions, brief and simple, as to how we should integrate the scriptures into our lives. It is a teaching that we gather from various places in the New Testament. There are a number of key passages, key words. Among them are: Listen and keep, Put into practice, Keep in mind, Ponder.

Listen and Keep
> Now as he was talking a woman spoke up in the crowd and said, 'Happy the womb that bore you and the breasts that you sucked'. But he replied, 'Still happier are they who listen to the word of God and keep it'. Lk.11:28.

The teaching is precise: Listen to the word of God and keep it. A little earlier Luke tells us:

> His mother and his brothers came to see him, but they could not get to him because of the crowd. He was told, 'Your mother and brothers are standing outside and want to see you.' But he replied, 'My mother and brothers are those who listen to the Word of God and put it into practice'. Lk.8:9 21.

Now we have an additional instruction: Listen and keep, yes, but put it into practice. Finally we have the advice: Keep and ponder in the heart. Listen, keep, put into practice, ponder in the heart. It is not by chance that all these actions are centred round Mary. St Anselm says: "She so listened to the word of God that it took flesh within her." Mary is the perfect model of one who listens, keeps

To Listen, Keep, and Ponder the Word

the word and puts it into practice in her life. She is the first disciple of Jesus. But she is also the model of one who ponders the word of God. Speaking of the Gospel of John, Origen says: "No one may understand the meaning of the Gospel, if they have not rested on the breast of Jesus and received Mary from Jesus, to be their mother also."

Our Lord's directions: Keep, listen, put into practice, ponder - their strength lies in their being found together. The quality of our lives as preachers will depend on the extent to which we have managed to unite them. Each instruction has its own lesson.

To Listen

It means to pay heed, to have an attentive ear. It means to be quiet. It was a custom in some Palestinian families that when a slave was received into a home the master of the house would take them over to the door and drive an awl through the lobe of the ear into the door post. The object of the exercise was to remind the slave that their job was to listen! In the Old and New Testament, hearing is more important than seeing. Seeing is good but for the biblical writers hearing is more important.

Why the primacy of hearing? Because God spoke. Yahweh speaks to his people. God's word is also creative. "He spoke and all things were made." The words "He said" are the first thing that we are told about God. Our relationship with God is a mouth to ear relationship. How often the prophets say: "Listen!" Each morning a Jew begins the Tephilah with the words: "Listen O Israel". Recall the number of times when Jesus begins preaching in parables and says, "Listen". What does the invitation to listen imply? Jaques Loew suggests it has three different levels of meaning.

It means - be Quiet

Silence, being quiet, is our way of helping God, so that he can come to us. Augustine explains: "God does not usually shout down the voices that clamour for our attention, we must silence them if we are to hear God's voice." Physical life needs movement and exercise. The spiritual life needs silence. But not any type of silence. It is not just an absence of noise and movement, nor is it a silence that is rigid, forced, or tension filled. It is the inner silence we experience when mind and imagination are at rest, the kind of silence the psalmist enjoins when he says: "Be still and know that I am God." Ps.46. Silence is not an exclusively Christian value. It is equally sacred in other religions, e.g. Hinduism, Buddhism...

It means - being at God's disposal

There are many levels of listening. We can listen out of curiosity as the

Growing in the Spirit of St Dominic

Athenians listened to Paul but with no interest in being changed, wishing only to be entertained by the art of the speaker. The attitude to which we are invited is to be open and at the disposal of God's word, willing to learn, willing to be changed, ready to receive and being open to the demands which the word makes upon us. It is a surrender to God's will.

It means Opening the Heart
This follows naturally from being quiet and being at God's disposal. We can listen, wait on God's word, be at God's disposal but it is God who opens the heart of each one. Jaques Loew gives the example of Paul's preaching to some women outside the gates of Philippi. Among the women was a certain Lydia. Luke says: "The Lord opened her heart to give heed to what was said by Paul". Acts 16:14.

To Keep
Listening leads to keeping. In Luke we read "and his mother kept all these things in her heart" 2:51. The literal translation is "carefully kept". It means careful and permanent storing in the memory. It reveals a frame of mind eager to understand the meaning of something, to hold it and reflect upon it until its full meaning is clear. Mary did not always understand but she kept all in her heart. How often she must have turned over passages of scripture in her mind drawing something new and deeper from them as she reflected over them again and again. You look at a picture or read a verse and at one glance capture all it has to say. Another picture, another verse, you return to again and again and each time are enriched. The same is true of the scriptures.

In an article "On Eating and Drinking the Word of God" Celine Mangan quotes from a piece with the same title by Caesarius of Arles:

> "For as the cows wander through the fields and the meadows and through the vineyards and the olive groves and from the leaves and grass they graze on provide milk for the calves, so ministers assiduously reading the Word of God on the wide hills of scripture, should from the herbage they gather provide spiritual milk for their children..."

Commenting on the passage she writes: "There is a real danger in our approach to the word of God as preachers and teachers that we become selective in what we take from the scriptures and work from a censored version of the Bible, or pick only the passages which represent the 'in' theology of the present moment. We need to sally forth from time to time into the highways and byways of the bible and sample the more unattractive sides of it. How often do we open a passage and say this surely has no relevance today, only to find in teaching... or at a prayer meeting, that it was the very text needed to open up whole new vistas for God's people."

Keeping the word is the work of sowing seed, allowing it to take root. It presupposes a climate in which it can germinate and become rooted in the heart. Once we have heard the word we must make it stay in us, not keeping it in cold storage but allowing it to grow through successive stages of our lives.

Pondering in the Heart
"Mary kept all these things, pondering them in her heart" Lk.2:19. The Greek word means to ponder over. It is a process which has been described as a gentle chewing of the word that slowly releases its inner riches. In Hebrew the word for pondering means murmuring, meditating. "How blessed the man... who finds his pleasure in the law of Yahweh, murmuring that over, day and night."

Word of God is Alive, it is Life
We read the scriptures to learn about God but we also come to the scriptures to be formed by God. Pondering the scriptures should lead us into the mind of Jesus for the world of today, not the world of yesterday. We never read the word in a vacuum. It has a message for our time, and our needs. We see this process at work in the lives of St Anthony of the desert (252-341) and Francis of Assisi (1296-1228). Both hear the same verse of scripture but their response differs. It was conditioned by the different historical social and cultural situations in which they found themselves.

John Paul II, referred to this process in a homily in Brazil 1980.

> "Since its beginning the Church has continually meditated on these passages and messages, but it is aware that it has not plumbed their depths as it would like… In varying concrete situations it rereads these texts and scrutinizes the message they contain, in the desire of discovering a new application for them."

Our experience is deeply coloured by our cultural environment, and the time in which we live. We live out our faith in a given concrete situation. Instead of trying to interpret a text with the mindset of the past we relate it to the reality in which we live and use the bible to throw light on this reality.
Finally, Vatican Council II, in particular the decree on Divine Revelation placed new emphasis on the place of the scriptures in Christian life.

> "The Church has always venerated the divine scriptures as she has venerated the Body of the Lord, in so far as she never ceases, particularly in the sacred

Growing in the Spirit of St Dominic

liturgy, to partake of the bread of life and to offer it to the faithful from the same table of the Word of God and the Body of Christ. Divine Revelation. No. 21"

The liturgy enhances our understanding of God's presence in the word proclaimed. Christ is present and speaks when the Gospel is read out. The liturgy makes this clear. The Alleluia verse before the Gospel is a welcoming of Christ into our community. When the celebrant says: "The Lord be with you", it is an expression of hope but also a reality. "The Lord is with you." We reply: "Glory to you Lord." Glory to you Lord Jesus present in our midst, in a way in which you have not been present before. The passage read out is not an account of what happened two thousand years ago. It is happening now. God is speaking to us and our world, today.

There is a different Gospel each day. While the whole Christ is offered to us in the Eucharist we are limited in our capacity to receive and so we grow step by step into the mystery of Christ throughout the liturgical year. The feast of the Nativity has a precise message and a special grace. The heart of Christ is open to us and comes to us at Christmas by way of the Christmas readings. The grace of the Christmas Gospel is not the grace of the Easter Gospel. The Readings, specify that aspect of the Mystery of Christ to be given to us in the word. Christ is present, and speaks when the word is proclaimed, and when we read the word.

Simon Roche, OP

This day,
I must keep the presence of my God,
I must walk with my God,
I must laugh with my God,
I must weep with my God,
I must talk with my God.

Lectio Divina
A New Spiritual Springtime

Where we have come from
Fr Joseph Prost CSSR was an Austrian who pioneered the Redemptorist parish missions in Ireland from 1851 to 1854. These missions were to prove of enormous significance for the practice of the faith in Ireland after the Famine. Historian Emmet Larkin maintains that the parish mission movement was the single most important factor in promoting the religious renewal, which took place in Ireland between 1850 and 1880. He says that in the space of a single generation the majority of the Irish people were transformed into the practising Catholics they have essentially remained until recent times. The first Redemptorist mission in Ireland was in the Cathedral Parish in Limerick. On the opening night Fr Prost told the people that the purpose of the mission sermons was to look at the Word of God so that their hearts would be saturated with it. Then he said: 'The Catholic Church has presented this Word of God in a small book, which is called the catechism.' Mrs. Monsell, a prominent Protestant, came to the mission one night when Fr Prost preached about Jesus and his Passion. She said that everything was fine but asked why the preacher had not encouraged his listeners to read about Jesus in the Holy Scriptures themselves.

Where we are Going
Notice how different Cardinal Martini's way of preaching the word of God is to Fr Prost's. For many years he taught young people in Milan to read the Scriptures for themselves and to meditate and pray with them. Here is an example. He read with them the story of the raising to life of the son of the widow of Nain. Then he asked them to reflect on the story. He drew their attention to one sentence: 'Young man, I tell you: get up.' He pointed out that Jesus says three things in that one sentence, and that each one deserves our full attention.

> **'Young man:'** Jesus addresses him first as one among the young people of his time – he belongs to a particular family in a particular cultural and religious community. Young people are conscious of belonging among their peers.

> **'I tell you:'** Jesus speaks to him as a unique person. What Jesus has to say now is directly for him and for him alone, and he knows that Jesus recognises and values him for who he is. He is not one of a crowd but a person with his own identity.

> **'Get up:'** Jesus tells him to get on his feet, to live his life to its fullest potential. Martini helps the young people to hear Jesus now addressing these

words directly to each of themselves, to ponder them, to find encouragement and inspiration in them, and to respond to Jesus in prayer.

This is *lectio divina*: reading the Scriptures, pondering them until they become like a mirror in which we see ourselves, our lives and our world reflected, and then responding to God in prayer.

Old and New
The two Latin words mean 'sacred reading' and they remind us that this is an ancient method that goes back to the first thousand years of Christianity; during that time it was the principal way of reading the Bible. The method went into decline but continued in monasteries. St. Dominic used it. In a thirteenth century document, which describes his Nine Ways of Prayer, lectio divina, was the eighth way. He would sit down by himself, recollect himself in the presence of God and read and pray, letting the words touch his mind as if he heard God actually speaking to him. "It was as if he was discussing something with a friend; ...at times he would listen quietly and discuss and argue, and then laugh and weep all at once, and fix his gaze and bow his head, speaking quietly again and beating his breast." He passed quickly 'from reading to prayer, from prayer to meditation, from meditation to contemplation."

Lectio divina has been rediscovered in our own time as people are learning to use it by themselves and in groups. There are two reasons for practising it. The first is to meet God in a personal way. The Vatican Council document on Revelation says that when we read the Scriptures, the Heavenly Father comes lovingly to meet his children and to converse with them. The second reason is to grow in wisdom: to come to understand God better, to understand ourselves and other people and the world in which we live. Fr Carlos Mesters has spent his life helping very poor communities in Brazil to read the Bible; he says that their concern is not to interpret the Bible, but to interpret their lives in the light of the Bible. In the Word of God they find the strength to keep going and not to give up the struggle.

The Bible is a Book of Stories, not a Book of Information
When God decided to give a book to humanity, he could have given us a book of information. Such a book would have been very useful. When we were puzzled about any of the big questions that arise in our lives we could look up the index and get the information we needed - about God, prayer, right and wrong, suffering, living in peace with others, life and death and the hereafter, and so on. To read such a book, we would use our minds to grasp the information. But God gave us a different kind of book: the Bible is for the most part a book of stories or narratives. A story engages our imagination. Then our feelings are touched

Lectio Divina

– we become excited or sad or angry or anxious. Another faculty that comes into play is our memory; a story reminds us of something in our own experience – something that has happened to ourselves or to people we know about.

Every story has characters, at least one; and it has movement, a plot. We identify with one or other of the characters. Some part of the plot may remind us of something in our own lives or in the lives of people we know about. Many who read the Bible read it as if it was a book of information; it may take time and practice to learn to read the Bible in a way that allows it to stir our imagination, touch our feelings and evoke our memories.

Lectio divina is done in three stages.

1. **Reading.**
   We choose a small portion of scripture and we read it over and over. Very often people choose to read the Gospel of the coming Sunday; they read it from the previous Monday all through the week. We read slowly and reverently. We give our whole attention to the words in front of us. We allow ourselves to enjoy the story, to grow to love the story and the words in which it is told. If something in the story puzzles us or seems to make no sense, we may need help from a commentary or from some one who knows more about the Scriptures than we do. It takes discipline to stay with one portion of Scripture, especially if it seems to say nothing to us for a long time.

2. **Meditation.**
   Reading flows naturally into meditation. We may do our meditation with the Bible in our hands. Likewise we may do it as we go about he activities of our day. At this stage our interest will focus on the present time and we ask: Where is this text happening in my life or in the world around me right now? In a natural and spontaneous way the answer will appear, either when something in the text reminds me of something that has happened in my experience, or something that has happened reminds me of the text. Suppose I am meditating on the words of Jesus at the Last Supper: 'No one has greater love than this: to lay down one's life for one's friend.' I ask myself: what does this remind me of ? Where have I seen this happening? In moments like this I am not waiting for the text to give me a message for my life, or to tell me what I should do. I am waiting for the text to evoke a concrete memory. I may remember a neighbour who has been looking after a sick relative with great generosity for a long time. I recognise that this person has been doing what Jesus spoke of... Or I read something in the papers that reminds me of the words of Jesus; in February, Francis Delaney risked his life to rescue two small children from a fire in their home in Thurles. As I continue to meditate

Growing in the Spirit of St Dominic

I may recall times I laid down my life for others in smaller ways. I see a pattern in the concrete memories that come to me: good people are willing to lay down their lives for others. I am touched by this and feel convinced that it is a wise way to live, and I am drawn to live in this generous way.

3. **Prayer.**
Prayer occurs spontaneously. In our meditation, when we are reminded of something in our experience, we are moved to pray. The prayer will be of three kinds:

- *thanksgiving:* when the text reminds us of goodness we have seen, we pray in praise and thanksgiving;

- *repentance* (or humility): when it makes us aware of the wrong we have done or the good we have failed to do, we ask for forgiveness;

- *petition:* when the text reminds us of our own needs or of the needs of others, we pray in petition.

If we stay long enough with our reading and meditating we may be led to a deeper moment of prayer in which we are no longer thanking or repenting or asking, but are leaving ourselves trustingly in God's hands. This is called contemplative prayer.

Pope Benedict spoke about lectio divina on 16th September 2006: "I would like to recall and recommend the ancient tradition of Lectio Divina: the diligent reading of Sacred Scripture accompanied by prayer brings about that intimate dialogue in which the person reading hears God who is speaking, and in praying, responds to him with trusting openness of heart. If it is effectively promoted, this practice will bring to the Church – I am convinced of it – a new spiritual springtime."

Brendan Clifford, OP

To Praise, To Bless, To Preach
Excerpt from the talk of Fr. Timothy Radcliffe

"To praise, To bless, To preach" is the title of Timothy Radcliffe's Letter to the Dominican Family. He uses as his text: "On the first evening of that day, the first day of the week, the doors being shut where the disciples were, for fear of the Jews, Jesus came and stood among them and said to them, 'Peace be with you'..."

John 20:19-23

I am convinced that if we can come to share a common preaching of the gospel, then it will renew the whole Order... All preaching begins with listening to the gospel... One cannot be a preacher without getting wounded. The Word became flesh, and was hurt and was killed. He was powerless in the face of the powers of this world. He dared to be vulnerable to what they might do to him. If we are preachers of that same word, then we will also get hurt. At the heart of the preaching of St Catherine of Siena was her vision of the wounded Christ, and she was given a share of his wounds. We may only suffer small wounds, being mocked, or not taken seriously. We may be tortured like our brother Tito de Alencar in Brazil, or killed like Pierre Chaverie in Algeria and Joaquin Bernardo in Albania... Everyone of us is a wounded preacher. But the good news is that we are preachers because we are wounded. Gerald Vann, an English Dominican, was one of the most famous writers on spirituality in the English speaking world since the Second World War. He struggled with alcoholism and depression all his life. That is why he had something to say. We have a word of hope and mercy because we have needed them ourselves... Every wound we have can become a door for the rising sun.

Being a preacher means that every one of us is sent from God to those whom we meet. A wife is sent to the husband and the husband to his wife. Each is a word of God to the other. The nun may not be able to leave the monastery, but she is just as much sent as any brother. She is sent to her sisters, and the whole monastery is a word of God sent to us. Sometimes we accept our mission by remaining where we are and being a word of life there. One of my favourite Lay Fraternities is in the Norfolk prison in Massachusetts, in the United States. The members of that fraternity cannot go elsewhere but they are preachers in that prison, sent to be a word of hope in a place of suffering. They are sent as preachers to a place which most of us cannot go.

Preaching in a pulpit has always been a small part of our preaching. In fact one could argue that Dominic wished to carry the preaching of the gospel out of the confines of the Church and into the street. He wished to carry the word of God to where people are, living and studying, and arguing and relaxing. For us the challenge is to preach in new places, on the Internet, through art, in a thousand ways. It would be paradoxical if we thought that preaching in the pulpit was the only real way of proclaiming the creativity of Dominic, a retreat back into the church.

We are all "good stewards of God's varied grace" 1 Peter, 4.10, in different ways. Each of us has received the grace of preaching, but differently. The Dominican martyrs in Vietnam, China and Japan in the seventeenth century were men and women, lay and religious, with an extraordinary diversity of ways of being a preacher. St Dominic Uy was a Vietnamese Dominican lay man who was known as "The Master Preacher", and so obviously he proclaimed the word; Peter Ching was a Chinese Lay man who took part in public debates in Fogan, to defend the truth of Christianity, just like Dominic with the Albigensians. But other lay Dominicans who were martyred were catechists, inn-keepers, merchants, and scholars… We preach the Word which has become flesh, and that Word of God can become flesh in all that we are, and not just what we say. St Francis of Assisi said: "Preach the gospel at all times. If necessary, use words!"… St Paul wrote to the Corinthians, "You are a letter from Christ delivered by us, written not with ink but with the Spirit of the living God, not on tablets of stone, but on the tablets of the human heart." In some situations the most effective word can be silence… The word also becomes visible in poetry and painting, in music and dancing. Every skill gives us a way of propagating the word…

I was at a meeting of the Dominican Family in Bologna earlier this year. Here Dominic is buried, but here his family is alive. There is a group of Laity who work with the sisters and brethren in preaching missions in parishes. There is another group of Laity and brethren whose love is philosophy, and who saw their mission as confronting the intellectual vacuum at the heart of people's lives. They preach by teaching. And there was a fraternity of Laity who said that they wished to support the mission of the others by praying.

We will therefore only flourish as a family of preachers if we make each other strong, and give each other life. We must breathe God's breath into each other, as Jesus did on the disciples. St Catherine of Siena was a preacher not just in what she said and wrote, but in giving others strength. When the Pope was getting discouraged, she stiffened his courage. When her beloved Raymond of Capua, the Master of the Order, was afraid, she encouraged him onwards. When a criminal was condemned to death, she helped him face execution. She says to him: "Courage, my dear brother, we shall soon be at the weeding feast… Never forget this. I shall be waiting for you at the place of execution."

The full text of Fr Timothy's talk is available in: To Praise, To Bless, To Preach, available from Dominican Publications. It is also found on the Internet at www.op.org/op Access documents.

Fra Angelico – A Word that Brings Hope

Fra Angelico was twenty, already painting and illuminating manuscripts when he and his brother Benedetto joined the Dominicans in 1407. Early in their work as painters both lost heart, wondering whether they should abandon their painting. Looking for guidance, they turned to Lawrence of Ripafratta who told them.

> "You will be none the less true Friars Preachers
> if you cultivate your painting
> for it is not only by preaching that we persuade people,
> but also by the arts,
> especially by music and painting.
> Many who will turn a deaf ear to preaching
> will be won by your pictures
> which will continue throughout the ages
> to preach."

Unfolding a Tradition

We ask you
To go out
And meet the poor Lazarus,
In his hunger and his misery.

Make yourself his neighbour,
So that he can recognise in
Your eyes, the eyes of Christ
Welcoming him…

So that you may relieve those who are
Most disinherited and share in the progress
Of the people who are most deprived.

Pope Paul VI

Love your neighbour,
observe the source of that love in you;
there as best you can,
you will see God.

St Augustine

Unfolding a Tradition

Compassion for the poor and the victims of injustice is woven into the Dominican tradition. A tradition we are called to continue. It takes two forms: relieving want and the causes of injustice.

The First Cry of the Poor - Relieving Want
Relieving want: "I was hungry and you gave me food, I was thirsty and you gave me something to drink, I was a stranger and you welcomed me, I was naked and you gave me clothing. I was sick and you took care of me. I was in prison and you visited me." Mt. 25:35-36. Relief of want has always been part of our tradition.

Jordan of Saxony, Dominic's successor, gave something to the first poor person he met each morning on the road. Often, he took off his tunic and gave it to a shivering beggar. His companions rebuked him and requested a General Chapter to tell him to stop it. Imagine, the Master of the Order going round half dressed! Catherine went to her father and begged him to grant her permission to give alms to the poor. "No one is to hinder my daughter in her alms giving." Her mother was not amused. Martin gave away his clothes and found room for the sick and homeless. When corrected for taking a sick Indian to his room he said: "I did not know that obedience came before charity," and when questioned about putting a dirty beggar in his bed he replied: "Compassion is better than cleanliness..."

In 1614 the Master of the Order described the giving of alms to the poor at the priory door as "a universal and inviolable custom in the Order." We see this in modern times in Bl Giorgio Frassati who devoted himself to the needs of the poor through his work in the St Vincent de Paul, and in the life of Agnes McLaren in her efforts to supply medical care on the missions.

The Second Cry of the Poor - Eradicating the Causes of Injustice
While simple giving is always necessary, it does not heal the causes of want or injustice. Mother Teresa of Calcutta noted: "We are in the slums and the slums are still there."

Identifying and healing the causes of want is also part of our tradition. Dominic, Pius V, Antoninus, Las Casas, Agnes McLaren, Joseph Lebret, Georges Pire, to mention a few, set out to identify the causes of want and heal them.

We see it in Dominic as a young student in Palencia. Imagine the panic as famine spread and the hungry stream into the city. Food and grain are hoarded, the pleas of the poor knocking on the door ignored. There is fear and guilt as people begin to die. The response of the young student is immediate. He resolved at once "to do all he could to relieve the want of the dying poor. He sold all his belongings, even his books… establishing a centre for almsgiving." Our wildest acts of charity never go beyond a certain prudence; we make some provision for the future. He sold everything, he became poor and in selling his books sacrificed the life of his mind. He started a charity, a place both to distribute and collect help and create an awareness of the needs of the victims of famine. His kindness moved others to join him. Years later, abandoned in the South of France, he appealed to these friends to come and join him in the preaching. They are numbered among his first companions.

Then, there is his concern for the prostitutes in Toulouse the victims of war. He opened a house. When support failed he appealed to the Pope to urge the people of the city to support the project. In a moving appeal Honorius III wrote to the people of Toulouse.

As a boy, Pius V, was a shepherd, as Pope he introduced laws protecting agricultural workers, provided funds to counter money lending, built orphanages for street children and when plague broke out organised help for the distribution of food, clothing, medicine and money, he himself going on foot to visit the sick and the dying.

St Antoninus embodies both traditions. His care for the destitute was a by-word in Florence but he also analysed the injustices committed in the name of commerce, trade, banking and international exchange, and the evil of monopolies. He saw that the economic system itself imposed poverty and urged the need for the redistribution of wealth.

Agnes McClaren pleaded with the Holy See on six occasions to permit religious sisters become doctors to minister to the needs of the poor in the Indian sub-continent and played a part in the foundation of the Medical Missionary Sisters.

A Voice Crying in the Wilderness
The story of Antonio Montesino and the first Dominican community in the Caribbean and their defence of the rights of the peoples of Central America against the exploitation of the conquistadors has lessons for today. Stephen Neill, the Protestant historian, captures the influence of Montesino's famous sermon preached in a straw thatched church on the island of Hispaniola.

> "On the Sunday before Christmas Day 1511, in the island of Hispaniola, a Dominican named Antonio de Montesino preached a sermon on the text 'I

Unfolding a Tradition

am a voice crying in the wilderness,' and raised a tumult which has not quite died away."

Its long term effects must count it among one of the most influential sermons ever preached. A twenty-six year old in the congregation wrote it down.

"Tell me by what right and with and with what justice do you keep these Indians in such cruel and horrible slavery? ... How can you keep them so oppressed and worn out, without giving them enough to eat, nor taking care of them in sickness, through the excessive work which you impose upon them, they fall ill and die or rather you kill them, in your desire to dig up and acquire gold every day... Are they not men? Have they not rational souls? Are you not obliged to love them as you love yourselves? Do you not understand? Do you not feel? ... Know this for sure, that in the state in which you are in, you cannot find salvation..."

He left everyone in a state of shock. It was the community who decided to make a stand. They sat together, wrote the sermon and chose Antonio to deliver it. He was the best preacher. It was a community decision. The young man in the congregation who took down the sermon was as angry as everyone else. Several years later he had a conversion, became a Dominican and for fifty years fought for the rights of the peoples of Central America. His name was Bartolome De Las Casas. Las Casas had the insight that Jesus is present in the poor.

"In the Indies I have seen Jesus Christ, our God, scourged and afflicted and crucified, not once but millions of times."

Gustavo Gutierrez reflects: "The reality of the poor in the time of Las Casas is the reality of the poor today though in other ways - exploitation, inferiority, lack of freedom..."

Linkage, A Lesson for Today
The great lesson for us today is that any success they had was the result of linkage. The authorities tried to silence Montesino. Get rid of the man, silence the voice. They failed because it was not just one person but a community and through linkage they built an articulate lobby of like minded people; lay people, theologians, people in the universities in Spain...

The Contemporary Scene
Continuing to spin this thread in the Dominican tradition we move to the 20th Century. Louis Joseph Lebret was a naval cadet in the First World War. In 1923 he became a Dominican. As a deacon and in poor health he was sent to

the seaport of San Malo to recover. The experience was to change his life. He made friends among the fishermen and their families, sat and listened to their stories and out of these meetings began to analyse the causes that imposed such hardship and degrading living conditions. Using the tools of social analysis, he examined the links between unemployment and the fishermen's starvation wage, between the chaotic local organisation of the fishing industry and the international efforts of large firms to monopolise the best fishing banks. This resulted in the passage of laws which helped to reorganise and restructure the French fishing industry.

In 1942 he founded "Economie et Humanisme." It developed into a centre for the study of social problems and for gathering teams with a variety of skills; agronomists, economists, theologians. Again, through the application of social analysis, Lebret and his companions pointed out the weaknesses inherent in both Western style capitalism and the monolithic centralised Marxist systems which stifled incentive. Pope Paul VI requested him to prepare a draft for the Encyclical Populorum Progressio, and "presented the Encyclical as a tribute to his memory."

Vincent Cosmao continued his work and broadened it in his contribution to the Synodal document on "Justice in the World," to which he contributed the section which states;

> "Action on behalf of justice and participation in the transformation of the world fully appear to us as a constitutive dimension of the preaching of the Gospel, or, in other words, of the Church's mission for the redemption of the human race and its liberation from every oppressive situation."

Working for justice is an essential part of evangelisation. It is never enough to preach justice, we must work for justice. Without this evangelisation is incomplete. This is after all the message of Dominic's life, Martin, Catherine, Giorgio Frassati and many others.

Georges Pire
In 1958, the Nobel Peace Prize was given to Georges Pire, a Belgium Dominican for his work for refugees. On the 27th February 1949 he attended a lecture given by a colonel Squadrille on the plight of refugees in Europe. At the end of the talk he requested the names of refugees for each member of his group. Thus was laid the foundations of an organisation which would assist 300,000 displaced persons living in camps and in sub-human conditions throughout Europe. Their purpose was to create homes for the elderly whom nobody wanted. From this developed "Europe of the Heart." Villages were established in Belgium, France, Germany,

Unfolding a Tradition

Austria, Greece... His answer to the question: Where will the money come from? "The good Lord will provide." Georges Pire, awakened Europe to the needs of the forgotten. What Can We Do?

Ally.
A conversation between Dr Marie McCormack, Michael O'Reagan. OP. and Fergal O'Connor OP. in 1961 prompted Fergal to start Ally to offer help to unmarried mothers in Ireland, through finding homes which would receive them for the duration of their pregnancy. Ally helped between 12,000 and 15,000 unmarried mothers. In 1972 he opened a hostel for homeless street girls.

St Martin de Porres Trust, Youghal.
Helps needy people through the sale of clothes, support for missions in Africa, Europe and the West Indies. Prepares a programme on local radio.

The Aids Fund Housing Foundation.
Provides accommodation and twenty four hour care for homeless people in the later stages of Aids illness. Fr Paddy McGrath is associated with the Aids fund project.

Conclusion
Dominic's compassion was shaped by his experience, first in his home and then as a student in Palencia and later as a preacher. He entered into the experience of the poor. Who were Dominic's poor? The victims of famine, slavery and war, the victims of material poverty and exploitation, prostitutes deprived of their dignity as human beings. But more, there was his compassion for sinners and those who had been led astray and lost contact with the Jesus of the Gospels, together with all those who had never heard the Word preached to them. These were Dominic's poor. He saw them, met them, sat, listened and spoke with them. They entered his life through the window of experience. Who are our poor?

Simon Roche OP

The Dominican Family

"In order that we may fully be 'ourselves' in the Order we are going to have to be Dominicans together... Could we not do and be much more, very much more, if we only reflected together more about the basis of our common vocation, and we shared in common all its riches - in that corner of the missions, or this neighbourhood of some large city, in this lecture hall of a university, or in this prayer group. What constitutes the Dominican family, is the Word of God prayed together, studied together, proclaimed together in the most complementary of temperaments, of vocations and the richness of persons..."

Vincent de Couesnongle

"Dominican spirituality, when it is known, attracts many women and men of today, especially young people. We cannot be in accordance with the apostolic priorities established by our General Chapters, unless we work together as friars, sisters, clerics and lay people, inspired by the zeal of St Dominic, so that we can respond to the challenge of the second millennium: to announce to all, in every place, Jesus Christ, friend and Saviour of humankind.

In the past perhaps, we have emphasised the diversity rather than the identity of the Dominican Family. This very diversity could be our strength, if it is placed at the service of the common charism, which consists essentially in that the Word of God is prayed in common and, above all, preached in common".

Mexico 1992

The Dominican Family

The "Dominican Family" is a modern term used to describe a reality which has roots at the very beginnings of the Order. The three branches - brothers, sisters and laity came into being almost simultaneously. In different ways, they worked for the Preaching. The Dominican Order was born a family. This has a particular interest and challenge for Lay Dominicans today.

The first foundation at Prouille', was a joint foundation with a prior and prioress. Apart from providing a refuge for young women, Dominic used it as a springboard for preaching" and a place to which the brothers might return and rest. The life of the sisters was devoted to prayer, asceticism and manual work through which they participated in the preaching of the brothers.

If Dominic worked hard to establish the men's foundations, he worked even harder to establish the sisters. He clearly saw that they fulfilled an indispensable role in the mission of the Order.

One of the outstanding examples of collaboration between sisters and brothers was the spiritual movement in Germany in the 13th and 14th century. It traced its origin to Albert the Great and his disciple Meister Eckhart, John Tauler, Margaret and Christine Ebner, and Henry Suso, and many others. The brothers passed on their theological learning to the sisters, and in their turn were nourished by the religious experience of the latter.

Lay Dominicans
Lay people also played a part from the very beginning. Vladimir Koudelka writes that on the 8th of August 1207, the same year as the foundation of the nuns, a group of lay people including married couples offered themselves and their property to Dominic and the preaching. Within twenty-five years of his death the Dominican family was formally expanded to include the Laity. The "Statute of Bologna" (1244) states that the purpose of such lay groups is: "to encourage those who are at enmity to make peace, to visit the fatherless and widows and orphans, the sick and prisoners and the poor and any others who are afflicted in any way, offering their loving service of help and advice;" words which evoke the activity of Catherine of Siena in the 14th century.

The Dominican Family Today
A renewed interest in the idea of the Dominican Family was initiated by two Masters of the Order at the beginning of the twentieth century: Hyacinth Cormier (1904-1916) and Bonaventure Garcia de Paredes (1926-1929). In his first letter to the Order, in 1927, Paredes described the Order as "a particular

and intimate family of the great Christian Family" and urged a strong family spirit among all its members. In the second half of the twentieth century, after the Vatican Council, this idea was taken up by a succession of General Chapters. The Chapter in 1968 at River Forest in the United States defined the Dominican Family as being:

> "composed of clerical and cooperator brothers, sisters, members of secular institutes and lay and priestly confraternities", and declared: "All the groups which comprise the Dominican Family share the same common vocation and each, in its own way, serves the mission of the Order in the world."

The Tallaght Chapter in 1971 urged that the laity of St. Dominic should be led to a more intimate connection with the Order and, a more profound commitment. The Chapter at Madonna dell' Arco in 1974 invited nuns, sisters, and lay Dominicans to take part, and abolished the terms First, Second and Third Order as terminology unsuited to contemporary society.

In the three years between Madonna dell Arco and Quezon City, the Commission on the Dominican Family wrote a document in which they called for united service. They expressed anxiety on two counts. They warned against the danger of family members going their separate ways and neglecting potential resources in the Order. Secondly, they expressed the need to reflect and act on two great movements of today: the emergence of the laity as an indispensable element in establishing the Kingdom of God, and the more recent and constantly growing movement towards the liberation of women and the recognition of their equality with men. The document also warns against the danger of becoming too inward-looking, for St Dominic created his family, not for itself but to be at the service of the Church and its mission in the world. It further reminds us of the vast resources within the family but adds:

> "We must admit that through lack of cooperation this tremendous potential is not fully realised, and the development of an authentic Dominican spirit and of Dominican spirituality has suffered. Now is the acceptable time for the Dominican Family to achieve true equality and complementarity among its different branches. If we believe that the Holy Spirit truly speaks to us in and through the signs of the times, we cannot ignore this call to develop among all the branches of the Order a greater collaboration in all its ministries... What lies before us at this time is a challenge to become what St Dominic had begun."

The Chapter at Quezon City in 1977 matched this statement by stating:

> "Non-clerical members of the Order are not less Dominican, nor do they participate in a defective way in the Dominican Vocation."

The Dominican Family

The Bologna Symposium of April 1983 brought together sisters, brothers, and lay Dominicans from all corners of the world and from all branches of the Dominican Family, in advance of the Chapter of Rome in 1983. The Chapter commended cooperation among all groups of the Dominican Family in the work of evangelisation, and exhorted the brothers "to continue or begin this cooperation with the other members of the Dominican Family ... in the ministry of the Word, in the direction of spiritual exercises, in movements of spirituality or youth groups, in catechises, in programmes of formation, in the promotion of vocations, and in works of justice and peace."

In Manila, in the year 2000 took place the first ever gathering of all branches of the Dominican Family - nuns, active sisters, friars and laity - with the aim of developing a common mission for preaching. This wonderful gathering showed the progress that had been made in the previous three decades. The theme chosen was "New Voices for the Millennium: The Dominican Family in Mission Together." Its declared goal was:

> "to celebrate the grace of Dominic and the joy of being in mission together, to make more acute our awareness of the hopes and sufferings of our world, to learn from each other in our diversity, and to dance together into the new century."

Four Masters
While many have contributed to the growth of the Dominican Family Spirit in modern times, there can be little doubt about the role played by Aniceto Fernandez, Vincent de Couesnongle, Damian Byrne and Timothy Radcliffe.

In his letter of 1968, Aniceto Fernandez caught the mood of the Order and the desire of the sisters, in particular, for closer ties within the Dominican Family. He enthusiastically supported this movement. This support was continued no less enthusiastically by his successor Vincent de Couesnongle, who returned repeatedly in his addresses and letters to the theme of the Dominican Family.

> "In order that we may fully be 'ourselves' in the Order, we are going to have to be Dominicans together... Could we not do and be much more, very much more, if we only reflected together more about the basis of our common vocation, and shared in common all its riches - in that corner of the missions or this neighbourhood of some large city, in this lecture-hall of a university, or in this prayer group!"

Elsewhere, he offered a definition: "What constitutes the Dominican Family is the Word of God, prayed together, studied together, proclaimed together in the complementarity of temperaments and of vocations, and the richness of persons." While remarking, in his address to the Chapter of Walberburg in 1980, that the entire Order was more and, more sensitive to the idea of the Dominican Family, he noted that there was some way to go: that this idea was much more alive with the sisters, and much less with the lay fraternities, and even less with the brethren.

Damian Byrne, elected in 1983, endorsed the movement, and gave it further emphasis in reflections he made on preaching and formation.

> A love of preaching should mark every Dominican priest, brother, sister and lay Dominican. With regard to preaching teams in the United States, I think that experience has been very positive. In many ways a priest is seen in a sacral role, whereas a sister and a lay person are seen as fellow Christians who are serious about the preaching of the Gospel and have nothing else to give but themselves and the Gospel. The priest is sometimes seen in a different role, and this very often diminishes his effectiveness as a preacher. I think that it is as communities of men and women that our preaching will be seen to be more effective, where the talents of everyone are used... It does mean that as a family we will have to preach and work together much more closely.

He makes the same point in a letter, "In Mission Together," addressed to sisters and brothers, urging collaboration in preaching.

> "We are called to be creative and flexible in preaching. If Catherine went to Raymond of Capua for spiritual direction, she in turn became his directress. A Dominican woman preaches the Word out of her experience of being a woman."

In May 1991 Damian Byrne met with the Dominican Superiors General at Santa Sabina in Rome, and spoke to them on the theme:" In Collaboration Together."

> "We Dominicans have a very precise identity. We are all preachers. This is our vocation. Everything in our lives is directed to this. We share this vocation, and I believe that we must as groups (not always as individuals) pursue our vocation together... If, indeed, we are a family, we should have much to share: insights, experience, a shared hope; we should inspire one another and dream a little together. There should be a cross-fertilization of experience and insight, a sharing with one another that is creative. But more, I believe, we should be sharing in ministry. We have begun, but we have only scratched the surface... I believe that it is only when we accept each other,

The Dominican Family

as equals that we can cooperate effectively together in ministry. This is the only basis for collaboration... Furthermore, we have to learn how to work with each other... to accept each other as, women and as men, as brothers and sisters. This requires a level of sensitivity and understanding not found in everyone."

Timothy Radcliffe's address as Master General to the Assembly at Manila is an inspiring reflection on the meaning of the Dominican Family. He began:

"When I was asked to address the Assembly of the Dominican Family, I was extremely excited. I am convinced that if we can come to share a common preaching of the gospel, then it will renew the whole Order." He went on to say: "Something new is happening. We must not be afraid. Wounded though we all are, we are all sent by God to preach, though not all in the same way. Together we have the authority to share the good news, whether from the pulpit or in a variety of other ways, which are all truly Dominican means of spreading the truth, of celebrating God's goodness. We need our Dominican Family to form us as human preachers, the laity contributing their own wisdom, other branches responding to the call to offer a full formation in theology and spirituality. Friendship, coupled with respect for others, is at the heart of Dominican spirituality.

Simon Roche, OP

The Journey

Formation

Our Dominican journey begins under the inspiration of the Holy Spirit, through contact with a Lay Dominican, another member of the Order, attendance at a Dominican Church, a book, or a pamphlet perhaps. This is the first step on our journey. When we decide to seek admission we are accompanied by another member for six months: a gentle, prayerful introduction to the Dominican Spirit.

Let us first remind ourselves of who we Lay Dominicans are: We are lay people who are Dominicans and members of the Dominican Order. Our inspiration is Dominic.

His mission was to preach Jesus Christ and bring the Gospel message to everyone, young and old and those who felt lost, confused or had gone astray. We form one family with the friars and the sisters.

We share in the apostolic mission of the Order and actively share in the life of the Church. We are a mixed bag of saints and sinners. We meet regularly to pray and study together and share each other's joys, problems, and hope. We reflect on the Word of God, seeking inspiration for our own lives and the lives of others. We preach in different ways, but each Lay Dominican receives the grace of preaching and exercises that grace in the way he or she lives.

If the Dominican project is preaching, how does a lay person participate in this mission? Fr Timothy Radcliffe explains: "Being a preacher means that every one of us is sent by God to those whom we meet. A wife is sent to her husband, a husband to his wife. Each is a word of God to each other." The members of the Dominican Chapter in Norfolk prison, Massachusetts are "sent to be a word of hope in a place of suffering... Preaching in a pulpit has always been a small part of our preaching... One could argue that Dominic wished to carry the preaching of the Gospel out of the confines of the Church into the street. He wished to carry the Word of God to where people are, living and studying, arguing and relaxing." Addressing the Dominican Family in Manila, fr Timothy quotes St Paul. "You are a letter from Christ... written not with ink but with the Spirit of the living God, written not on tablets of stone, but on the tablets of the human heart."

St Catherine of Siena was a preacher not just in what she said and wrote, but in giving others strength. When the Pope lost courage she helped to stiffen his resolve. "To affirm others with a word or a smile is to preach. To be present to

The Journey

those who mourn is to preach. In some situations the most effective word may be silence! What you are, is a preaching."

Preparation for Admission - The Guide
If you are chosen by your chapter to be the guide of a new member the following may be helpful. First, it may help to spend a little time reflecting on your own formation. What helped you at the beginning of your own journey? Share your own story with the candidate. Each person is a gift from God, each is unique. The Divine spark in each is different. We can truly say, "I am the only one". As each of us reflects a different facet of the Divine, our needs differ. Have the courage to be guided by the Spirit during these months. Move at the pace of the new member not your own. The spirit of Dominic is more likely to be caught from someone than from a book. Just as the spirit of Moses was shared with the seventy two and as Elisha asked Elijah for a double share in his spirit, we ask for a share in the spirit of Dominic, the Spirit of Jesus as manifested in Dominic's life. Let us begin with a warm welcome and a prayer to Dominic: A prayer of your choice or perhaps the following.

Prayer
0 wonderful hope, which you gave to those who wept for you at the hour of your death, promising after your departure to be helpful to your brothers and sisters. R/ Fulfill, father, what you have said and help us by your prayers.

You who shone by so many miracles worked on the bodies of the sick; bring us the help of Christ to heal our sick souls. R/ Fulfill, father, what you have said and help us by your prayers.

> Lord, let the holiness and teaching of Saint Dominic
> come to the aid of your church.
> May he help us now
> with his prayers as he once inspired people by his preaching.
> We ask this through Christ Our Lord.
> Amen.

Guide and Candidate
Each meeting is a weaving of prayer, study and discussion in not more than forty minutes. Depending on the candidate, the first meetings might be one to one, before an introduction to the chapter meetings. If your Chapter celebrates Evening Prayer at the beginning, the guide and candidate might join them and then leave to continue their session together.

Growing in the Spirit of St Dominic

What should we try to do during these first months? Ask for the grace of Dominic to follow Jesus in his spirit. That spirit, as mentioned already, is not easily caught from a book. Rather it is something that is caught from someone, and for us that someone is Dominic himself or those who are imbued with his spirit. You will discover that many Lay Dominicans are the living presence of Dominic for the world of today.

How should these sessions be conducted? We are not studying for an exam but that both may be touched and guided by Dominic's spirit in the following of Jesus today. You might dip into this little book in the following sessions according to the outline given here. There should be time for questions and discussion.

Session: 1 Welcome. Prayer to St Dominic
Reading: The Short life of St Dominic,
reading and praying a psalm each day.

Session: 2 Welcome. Prayer to St Dominic
Read: The Prayer of the Church (short version)
Ask the candidate to pray a psalm each day and
read the short life of St Catherine and begin the first three sections of: "Rediscovering our Dominican Charism" ending with "The Personal Following of Jesus."

Session: 3 Welcome. Prayer to St Dominic
Discussion of the reading, queries which may have arisen.
Reading: The remaining portion of "Rediscovering..."
Say Morning or Evening Prayer with the candidate or chapter. Encourage the candidate to say morning or evening prayer each day.

Session: 4 Welcome. Prayer to St Dominic
Discussion of the reading.
Read: Article on Lectio.

Session: 5 Welcome. Prayer to St Dominic
Read "To Listen, Keep and Ponder the word."

Session: 6 Welcome. Prayer to St Dominic
Discuss the reading.
Preparation session for admission: Handbook.

The Journey

Ceremony of Admission

We celebrate this decision at Mass, or during prayer at the Chapter meeting. As he was dying, Dominic promised to be of more help to us after his death than when he was alive. He will be your companion on your journey. Dominic's promise is embodied in the prayer being said at the beginning of each session.

Formation after Admission

We continue the journey. We have now begun to familiarize ourselves with the life of Dominic and Catherine. Together, during the coming months let us try to deepen the understanding of our Dominican calling.

Session: 1	Welcome. Evening Prayer with the Chapter. In the one to one session begin by addressing any questions the candidate may have. Read and discuss together the beginning of the section "To Praise, To Bless, To Preach." Ask them to re-read it for the next session.
Session: 2	Welcome. Discuss the material read since the previous meeting. Study the section on "Unfolding a Tradition." Complete the reading of it for next session. Encourage them to read one of the short lives of the Dominican saints or the short story of an outstanding Lay Dominican.
Session: 3	Welcome. Discussion. Begin: "Dominicans at Prayer". Complete it for the following session.
Session: 4	Welcome. Discussion. Begin "The Dominican family" Reflect on it for the next session.
Session: 5	Welcome. Discussion. Begin "Dominic: This is my Story". Reflect on it for the next session.
Session: 6	Welcome. Discussion "This is my Story". Preparation for Making of Promise.

This suggested outline must to be adapted to the needs of each candidate. Each session is a weaving of prayer, study and reflection.

At the end of the book you will find a short bibliography and a guide to accessing a reservoir of Dominican material on the web. Its use will depend on the time that each person can devote to reading and study. It is something to keep in mind for the future.

Growing in the Spirit of St Dominic

The Nine Ways of Prayer of St Dominic

Dominic's use of the body in prayer is found in the "Nine Ways of Prayer", ways of cultivating God's presence. They are recorded in a number of manuscripts. Leonard Boyle dates the beautifully illustrated manuscript in the Vatican library (Rossi 3) to c1325-1329.

First Way of Prayer
Dominic bows before an altar as though Jesus is personally present. He taught the brothers to do this, quoting from Ruth: "the prayer of the humble has always been pleasing to you." He taught them to venerate the cross in this way and to bow when they said the Gloria Patri.

Second Way of Prayer
His second way of prayer was to lie face down saying: "O God, be merciful to me, a sinner." Luke 18:13. With devotion and reverence he repeated the verse of David: "I am he who has sinned, I have done wickedly." He taught the young brothers that if they were unable to weep for their own sins there were many who need God's mercy.

Third Way of Prayer
Rising from the ground Dominic would do penance using the discipline in the manner of the time: penance for his own sins and the sins of others.

Fourth Way of Prayer
Dominic remained before the altar looking at the Cross frequently genuflecting, rising and kneeling, praying for sinners. He had deep confidence in God's mercy for himself, sinners, and for the ministry of the younger brothers whom he sent out to preach.

Fifth Way of Prayer
Sometimes when he was in house he would stand before the altar, his hands open, extending them, or joining them or at times lifting them to the level of his shoulders as if in conversation. When he was on the road he would steal away, and standing still utter a verse of scripture.

The Nine Ways of Prayer

The Sixth Way of Prayer
Dominic often prayed with his hands outstretched in the form of a cross. This is how he was remembered praying over the young man who was restored to life at St Sixtus in Rome. He practised this way of prayer on special occasions when he sensed something unusual was about to happen. He would say some verses from the psalms "O Lord, the God of my salvation: I have cried in the day and in the night before you... ".

The Seventh Way of Prayer
He was often found standing erect, stretching his whole body, his hands joined and raised towards heaven, like an arrow from a bow. Sometimes, he would open his hands as though receiving something. The brothers would hear him praying aloud and saying: "Hear, O Lord, the voice of my prayer when I pray to you, when I lift up my hands to your holy temple" Ps. 27:2.

The Eight Way of Prayer.
After saying the office and after meals Dominic hurried away to some quiet place. There he would make the sign of the cross, open a book and read. To those who observed him it seemed as though he heard Our Lord speaking. At other times it appeared as though he was arguing with a friend. At times it seemed he was somewhat impatient in his thought and words and then in the next moment he would become a quiet listener, then again he would appear to discuss and contend. He seemed almost to laugh and weep at the same time, and then, attentively and submissively, would murmur to himself and strike his breast and cover his face with his hands.

The Ninth Way of Prayer
Dominic spent a great deal of time on the road. Journeying through lonely areas he loved to fall behind his companion or go ahead a little to be with the Lord. He would say to his companion: "Let us go on and think of the Saviour". The brothers thought that it was on these journeys that Dominic developed his understanding of the scriptures. Frequently, on such journeys he sought protection by making the sign of the Cross.

Note:
The Nine Ways of Prayer of Saint Dominic, the facsimile edition of the Vatican manuscript with splendid reproductions of the original pictures is available from

Growing in the Spirit of St Dominic

Dominican Publications, Dublin. Translation by Leonard Boyle. It is expensive. Simon Tugwell's translation in pamphlet form is available at Santa Sabina, Rome. The Nine Ways of Prayer are featured on the internet and may be had through accessing "The Nine Ways of Prayer".

The Ascenion

There is no bird
you say
no sound
but sighing wind.

Yet absence
dances there
where I have seen
the bare
branch quiver.

There remains a tree
the trembling twig
love's weight
remembering.

The bird
has passed his flute
to the wind
this dance
will not be stilled.

Claire O'Connell

Devotion: The Prayer of the Church

The following is a brief introduction to the Prayer of the Church.

What is it?
The Prayer of the Church is the Church's official prayer and continues the prayer of Christ. More precisely, it is the prayer which Jesus himself, together with his Body the Church, addresses to the Father.

Jesus prays in us
It is not just "I" or "You" who make this prayer. When "I" pray the office, it is Christ, the head of the Body the Church, who prays in me and through me. Christ prays to the Father through his Spirit in us.

This has profound implications. The prayers of petition, praise and thanksgiving which we make in the psalms are not just our prayer, they are the prayer of Jesus. St Augustine says: "Jesus prays for us as our priest, he prays in us as our head." At Baptism we become members of his body, he the Head we the members. As head of the body, Jesus prays in us. We never pray alone. We pray in the name of Jesus and in the name of each of his members.

And here is the secret of this Prayer. It is not so much a question of understanding the words that are to be said but of appreciating the One who is praying them in us. It is not so much a matter of stirring up our own personal devotion but of putting on the devotion of him in whose name the prayer is said. It is his prayer that we say from the book of the hours. I am part of the vine that is Christ.

The dignity of this prayer arises from the fact that it is the Prayer of Christ. It is not a private prayer. Private prayer tends to focus on ourselves, our needs and concerns. The Prayer of the Church has for its concern the needs of the whole Church and the world. In this prayer, we lend Christ our tongue and heart to pay a tribute of praise and thanksgiving to God and to pray for the graces and needs of the Church, its members and the whole human race. And so it is not the prayer of an individual or even of a collection of individuals but the Prayer of the Church. The Church invites us to unite ourselves with her and with Jesus in this prayer.

Morning and Evening Prayer are the main hours. One sanctifies the morning the other the evening. In Psalm 5:4-5 we read: "I say this prayer to you, for at daybreak you listen for my voice." Evening Prayer sanctifies the end of the day. "We pray and beg that his light may shine on us again."

Why the Psalms
The Psalms are the inspired prayer of the people of God. Composed at different times, they include prayers of praise, petition, and thanksgiving. We have reason to believe that at all the critical moments in his life, even on the Cross, Jesus prayed the psalms or portions of them. They were part of his prayer.

Please keep in mind that every psalm has a particular application: Praise of God, the needs of the down-trodden, people in trouble, persecution, illness, broken families... It is the prayer of the whole Church, the cry of the broken, those filled with joy... This may be a little off-putting as the psalms do not always reflect our own mood! They were never intended to. I suppose, it is the problem of keeping our hearts in tune with what our lips are reciting. Time may help us to make them the vehicle of personal prayer.

We make this prayer for the Church and the whole of humanity. The Decree on the Liturgy reminds us that whenever this prayer is said: "it is the very prayer which Christ himself together with his body addresses to the Father."

The Prayer of the Church

Morning and Evening prayer follow a four week cycle.

Both, begin with a salutation followed by a hymn.

Then follows an antiphon which is said before and after each psalm - different antiphons for different seasons.

On the completion of the psalms there is a reading followed by a moment of silence to reflect on the reading.

Then follows a one line versicle, another antiphon and the Benedictus at Morning Prayer and Our Lady's Song, the Magnificat, at Evening Prayer. Finally, there are petitions and a concluding prayer.

Morning and Evening prayer are recited publicly by Benedictines, Cistercians, Carmelites, Dominicans, and others. In the beginning it may help to join them at prayer.

Devotion

The Rosary

The Rosary is a Gospel prayer centred on the life of Jesus. It moves through the life of Jesus: His childhood - the Joyful Mysteries. His public ministry - The Mysteries of Light. His suffering and death - The Sorrowful Mysteries. Finally, His Resurrection and Ascension with the coming of the Holy Spirit and Mary's Assumption and Coronation - The Glorious Mysteries. We read in the Gospels as Jesus passed by people stretched out their hands to touch him. In each mystery we can say that Jesus is about to pass by.

John Paul II suggested that the Joyful be said on Monday and Saturday, the Mysteries of Light on Thursday, the Sorrowful on Tuesdays and Fridays and the Glorious on Wednesday and Sunday.

The Joyful Mysteries: Monday and Saturday

- **The Annunciation**
  Mary is invited to become the Mother of God. "I am the handmaid of the Lord, be it done unto me according to your word."

- **The Visitation**
  Mary sets out in haste to be with her cousin Elizabeth.

- **The Birth of Jesus**
  I bring you good news of great joy. "The Word was made flesh and dwelt among us."

- **Presentation**
  Mary and Joseph present Jesus in the Temple.

- **The Finding of Jesus in the Temple**
  For three days Mary and Joseph search for Jesus and find him in the Temple.

The Sorrowful Mysteries: Tuesday and Friday

- **The Agony in the Garden.**
  "And being in an agony he prayed the more earnestly.

- **The Scourging at the Pillar**
  Now they mocked him, beat him and blindfolded him.

- **Jesus is Crowned with Thorns**
  The soldiers twisted some thorns into a crown and put it on his head. They came up to him saying "Hail, king of the Jews".

- **Jesus carries the Cross**
  Pilate handed him over to them to be crucified. They then took charge of Jesus, and carrying his own cross he went out of the city.

Growing in the Spirit of St Dominic

- **The Crucifixion**
  Jesus is crucified. "Father, into yours hands I commit my spirit."

The Mysteries of Light: Thursday
In these mysteries we join Jesus in his public ministry. He is the Light of the world.

- **The Baptism of Jesus in the Jordan**
  "This is my beloved Son, with whom I am well pleased." At his baptism the heavens open and the voice of the Father declares Jesus is his beloved Son. The Spirit descends upon him and sends him on his mission.

- **The Wedding at Cana**
  Jesus changes water into wine thanks to the intervention of Mary. He opens the hearts of the disciples to faith. He is a God of abundance.

- **Proclamation of the Kingdom of God and Conversion**
  It is by his preaching that Jesus proclaims the coming of the Kingdom. He calls us to conversion and forgives sin.

- **Transfiguration**
  The glory of the Godhead shines forth from the face of Jesus as the Father commands the astonished Apostles to "listen to him" preparing them for his Passion.

- **The Institution of the Eucharist**
  The final mystery of light is the institution of the Eucharist, in which Jesus offers us his body and blood as food.

The Glorious Mysteries

- **The Resurrection**
  When he rose early on the first day of the week, he appeared first to Mary Magdalene.

- **The Ascension**
  "This Jesus who has been taken up from you into heaven, will come in the same way."

- **The Coming of the Holy Spirit**
  "When the Counsellor comes, the Spirit of Truth, who proceeds from the Father, he will be my witness and you also will be my witnesses."

- **The Assumption**
  Mary the Mother of God, was taken body and soul to heaven.

- **Coronation**
  Mary is crowned Queen of Heaven.

Devotion

A Prayer of Two Words

"Mary stood at the tomb, outside, crying. As she wept, she bent down into the tomb, and she saw two angels in white, sitting one at the head and the other at the feet where the body of Jesus had lain. And they said to her, "Woman why are you crying?" She said to them, "They have taken away my Lord and I do not know where they have laid him." Saying this she turned and saw Jesus standing, but she did not know that it was Jesus. Jesus said to her, "Woman, why are you weeping? Whom do you seek?" She, thinking that he was the gardener, said to him." "Sir, if you have removed him, tell me where you have laid him, and I will take him away." Jesus said to her, "Mary." She, turning, said to him in Hebrew, "Rabbouni, which means "Teacher."

Jn. 20:11-16

The Resurrection meeting of Mary Magdalene and Jesus suggests a way of prayer. Thinking him to be the gardener she asks where Jesus might be? He says: "*Mary.*" Immediately, she recognises him and says: "*Rabbouni.*"

All the love that is in their hearts for each other is expressed in two words, Mary and Rabbouni. Other words are unnecessary. It suggests a way of prayer.

Gently, murmur the name "*Jesus.*" Let it resound in you. Repeat it after a space of several breaths. There is no hurry. Again, let it gently resound within.

Now say the name "*Jesus*" again. This time do not repeat it but after the space of a breath or two say your own name, *Anne/Peter*. Continue this very gentle rhythm. "*Jesus*" pause "*Anne*". A way of entering into presence.

It lends itself to prayer for others. This happens when you replace your own name with that of someone for whom you wish to pray. We place them and their need before Jesus.

It becomes a prayer for **peace** when the rhythm is "**Jesus**" "**Peace**." It becomes a prayer of **praise** when you substitute a word of praise. A key to this way of prayer is its quiet unhurried rhythm. Allow the name of Jesus to fall gently within you. Do not hurry. The rhythm of time and words creates calm leading into presence. Jesus present to you – you present to him.

The name of "**Jesus**" can be replaced with that of "**Father**," "**Spirit**," "**Mary**" or one of the saints.

A way of prayer which may be helpful when you are tired, a springboard to further prayer

Simon Roche, OP

Growing in the Spirit of St Dominic

Anne's Dream

"I had a dream, a beautiful dream. I was in a cedar wood house, it was round with no corners and when I left the house I carried the aroma of cedar wood with me, but the further I went from the house, the fainter the aroma of the cedar wood. It was as though I had to return to the house to replenish the smell of the cedar wood. One day many weeks later I had this word from the Lord: "You are loved at the centre of your own house."

The Boy

With my heart's eye
I see a lad
Lonely on a hillside
Learning
That he is not alone.

Like a leaping flame
the lesson
burns through generations
to lap my life
Patrick I thank you.

Claire O'Connell,

Devotion
The Divine Smile

When St Therese of Liseaux was ten years old she was cured of a serious illness by an apparition of Our Lady, radiantly beautiful. "But," wrote the saint, "it was her smile that pierced my heart."

The Scriptures often speak of the "smile" of God in order to express the gracious love and care he has for us: "May God be merciful to us and bless us; May he grant us the favour of his smile." All the Saints, like Our Lady, reflect on their countenance the loving smile of God that is revealed to us through Christ and the nearer they approach to God the more beautiful is this reflection.

What people remembered most vividly of St Catherine of Siena was her wondrous smile. It was the same with Bernadette, with Therese and many other saints, as if it were a special mark of God's chosen friends. Of Edel Quinn it was said that "she was always smiling, and her smile was something to remember. It was bright and frank, wholly attentive and understanding; it shed light around her."

If our nearness to God, our holiness, is often revealed by the quality of our smile, it is also true that we can draw very close to God by the mere effort to keep smiling for his sake. That sounds almost too simple a recipe for holiness. Simple it is but not always easy. There can be her self-effacement behind a smile, heroic faith and hope and charity. And it must surely lead to God since it comes from him, for every true smile is but a reflected ray of his eternal joy and love.

Anselm Moynihan, OP

The Laughter of God

Meister Eckhart reflects: "God enjoys himself. His own enjoyment is such that it includes his enjoyment of all creatures" Eckhart has this intuition that laughter is at the very heart of the Trinity: "the Father laughs at the Son and the Son at the Father and the laughing brings forth pleasure and the pleasure brings forth joy, and joy brings forth love." "This joy is near you, it is in you" find it, discover it and rejoice in it.

Growing in the Spirit of St Dominic

Truth

What is the strongest thing in the world? asked a king of his wise men. "Pleasure" answered some. "Power" declared others. Then one stood up and said: "No. the strongest thing in the world is Truth." It is not always easy to see that. There are times when Truth seems to be the weakest thing in the world. It seemed like that when Our Lord was crucified. Yet he rose from the dead.

To love the truth is what is asked before all things; it leads to strength and nobility of character, it brings us straight to God.

To love the truth means that I want, at all costs, to see things straight, as they really are. Then it could be said of me, as it was of Abraham Lincoln: "His thoughts were roots that gripped the granite truth."

To love the Truth means secondly that no lie ever passes my lips. My words, like my thoughts, will always correspond to things as they really are.

To love the Truth means not only knowing it and speaking it but building my life on it. I must have the Truth of life which means my life must be exactly what God wants it to be. I will be truly myself if I correspond perfectly to the particular idea which God has for me personally. How can I do that? By seeking nothing but God's will, moment by moment, in the little things that make up my day. Brick by brick I build the house of my life on the rock of Truth.

To love the truth means also that I seek to spread it. I try to pass on to others my own knowledge of God the Supreme Reality.

To know the truth, to speak the truth, to live the truth, to spread the truth is to walk in the way of holiness.

Anselm Moynihan, OP

It pertains to the virtue of truth,
not only to speak the truth,
but to speak it at the right time.

Thomas Aquinas

Short Lives

- St Dominic
- St Catherine of Siena
- St Martin de Porres
- Pier Giorgio Frassati
- Jonathan W. Nobles
- Agnes McLaren
- Honoria Magaen and Honoria Burke

St Dominic

"Childhood is the rib cage about which the shape of life is formed." It is certainly true of Dominic. He was born in the village of Calaruega in Northern Spain, on the frontier between Christianity and Islam, hot summers, piercing cold winters. All the family was affected by his mother's concern and care for the poor. His brother Anthony started a house to offer hospitality to tramps, pilgrims, and people of the road.

An uncle taught him a love of the psalms and the prayer of the Church. At fourteen he went to Palencia for a secular education and then the study of theology. In the beginning he lived in a hostel, then in his own room.

Famine was a frequent visitor to the region. One year the harvest failed and people streamed into the city in search of food. As food grew short the pleas of those knocking on doors was ignored. Food and grain were hoarded. There was fear and guilt as people began to die in the streets.

Our wildest acts of generosity never go beyond a certain prudence; we make some provision for the future. Dominic sold everything and became poor himself. He sold his books, his prized possession. In the 13th century a book was as valuable as a good cow or a small car. He said: "How could anyone study on dead skins when people were dying of hunger." He didn't give everything away in one dramatic gesture, he started a charity, to serve the needs of the starving. Other students and some of the Masters joined him.

His heart was set on being a priest and when he received an invitation to join the cathedral chapter at Osma he accepted. Ordained, he looked after the preaching in the cathedral. Then an event took place which was to shape the future of his life. Bishop Diego asked him to accompany him on a visit to northern Europe on behalf of the king. It changed both their lives.
In Northern Europe they came in contact with peoples who had not yet been evangelised and it sparked in their hearts a desire to be missionaries. On the return journey they visited Rome and Diego asked Pope Innocent III to relieve him of responsibility for the diocese of Osma so that they might become missionaries in Northern Europe. He refused.

Saddened, they set out for Spain. One morning or evening in June 1206 they reached the town of Montpellier in the south of France. As they entered the town they met the papal legates setting out to preach to the Albigensians. The legates were dispirited, making no progress, they sought the advice of Bishop Diego who suggested that their method of preaching was flawed.

Short Lives

Diego offered to lead them. They accepted and so began the Preaching of Jesus Christ. Two by two, on foot, they set out to evangelise. For two years Diego and Dominic preached throughout the region. Then the bishop returned to Spain to make arrangements for his diocese. Reaching Spain, he suddenly died. Dominic's friend and inspiration was dead. It threw the preaching into turmoil. Dispirited, all the missionaries returned home. Dominic, alone, remained. With bishop Diego he had founded a true Gospel way, a way of living poorly, praying and preaching Jesus Christ. There was a sense of loneliness and abandonment. Dominic determined to remain and continue what they had begun together. He made his headquarters in the small hill town of Fanjeaux where he lived in a stable. Often, he would go to a little promontory to pray. Below the town, the great plain stretched to the horizon – controlled by the Albigensians. If he turned he could see the Pyrenees mountains and beyond the mountains, Spain and home. Did he ask himself will I also go home? A poignant time. He stayed. He wrote to his friends who had helped him during the famine asking some of them if they would now join him in the preaching. Some did. They formed the nucleus of a new preaching mission. As early as the 8th of August 1207 a group of lay people including married couples offered themselves and their property to the preaching.

What was he like? Small 5.5", thin, like all Dominicans! Handsome, hair and beard slightly reddish, beginning to grey. A deep voice. But what was he like? With a certain humour Simon Tugwell wrote of him: "Contrary to the previous tradition of religious life, Dominic believed in the virtue of laughter." A happy man, with a sense of humour who could laugh at himself. Kind and cheerful, full of friendliness. Dominic was one of a new type of saint that appeared towards the end of the 11th Century for whom joyousness of heart outwardly expressed was felt to be a Gospel characteristic. Spontaneous in his ways, compassionate to those in need of any kind.

Who were Dominic's poor? The victims of famine, slavery, and war, the victims of material poverty deprived of their dignity as human beings but more, there was compassion for sinners and those who had been led astray and lost contact with the Jesus of the Gospels together with those who had never heard the Gospel preached to them. He saw them, met them, sat, listened and spoke with them. They entered his life through the window of experience.

At Toulouse, he made friends among the prostitutes, the victims of war. He turned to the bishop who had once been a troubadour, a sort of medieval hippie going round with his mandolin before becoming a priest and bishop. He gave Dominic a house. Yet in spite of the bishop's generosity and Dominic's scrounging, support was inadequate. Money was scarce but possibly there was another reason, the prudish scepticism of people. Dominic refused to take no for an answer. He went straight to the top and appealed to the Pope, Honorius

Growing in the Spirit of St Dominic

III, who responded by making a touching appeal to the people of Toulouse to support the foundation. This was Dominic. As the preaching mission grew, the number of his companions increased and he made Toulouse the centre of the preaching. Then, suddenly, he dispersed his first companions, some to Paris, others, to Spain and Italy. They were stunned as were his friends. One of his young companions John of Spain a critic and rebel refused to go unless Dominic gave him money for the journey! After Dominic's death John was the first to be called to give evidence at the process for his canonisation. He spoke movingly of Dominic, the man of prayer. He had a special prayer "that God would grant him true charity which would be effective in winning salvation for others." On the road he would frequently turn to his companion and say: "Let us go on and think of the Saviour". Then Dominic would fall behind to be with the Lord. He gave his companions a love for preaching and the word of God, his own devotion to the humanity of Jesus and his passion for the personal following of Christ.

A joyous tranquil spirit, spontaneity, the personal following of Jesus with all that this entails, an openness to new ideas and charisms, study in the service of the gospel, an ability to read the signs of the times and a carefully guarded apostolic freedom that enabled him to respond to the challenges of his day all characterised Dominic's spirit and are our inspiration for today.

Simon Roche, OP

I am the Father of Two Sons
Raymond of Capua, Catherine's confessor and friend, records an extraordinary vision in which Catherine sees the Father begetting the Son. Then the Father speaks of Dominic.

> "Dearest daughter, I am the Father of these two sons; of the One by natural generation; of the other, by loving and affectionate adoption… This Son who is mine by natural and eternal generation, was most perfectly obedient to me in all things, even unto death, in the human nature which he assumed. So too, Dominic, this son of mine by adoption, shaped every act he did, from his infancy till the last day of his life, by obedience to my commandments. Never once did he disobey a command of mine… and he preached not only in his own person, but through others also; not only in his own lifetime, but through those who followed him. Through these followers the voice of Dominic's preaching is heard today, and will continue to be heard. For just as my Son by nature sent his disciples to preach, so did Dominic, my adopted son, send out his friars… just as my Son by nature is my very Word, so this adopted son is the herald and the bearer of my Word. And so my special gift to him and his friars is understanding of the words I have spoken, and the grace of never swerving from them."

Raymond of Capua: *Life of Catherine*

Short Lives

St Catherine of Siena

St Catherine is the most celebrated Lay Dominican, and a source of inspiration. What does she say to us for today?

First, a brief glance at her early life. A twenty fourth child, a home full of noisy mischievous children, Catherine loved her family, loved her nephews and nieces. She was warm and affectionate.

Returning home with her brother Stephen after a visit to her sister Bonaventura, Catherine looked up and saw Jesus accompanied by Peter, Paul and John the Evangelist over the Dominican Church. He smiled and blessed her.

At fifteen years, she overheard plans for her marriage, she said: No. Her mother, Mona Lappa, turned to Thomas Catherine's adopted brother, a Dominican, in the hope that he would talk sense to her. Little did she know!

Faced with Catherine's adamant rejection of marriage Thomas suggested she might become a nun. Catherine said: No. She wanted to serve God in prayer at home. In jest Thomas suggested she might cut off her hair. "Then they will realise that you mean business." She did.

The family were furious. How dare she! Work was heaped on her, there was no time or even a place where Catherine could pray. Adversity was the source of inspiration. Guided by an impulse of the Holy Spirit, Catherine made herself a secret cell within her own heart where she could remain with the Lord.

Raymond of Capua her confessor and spiritual guide recalls how she would often say to him, especially, when he was involved in too much business or when he had to go on a journey: "Build yourself a cell within your own heart and never put a foot outside it."

As she urged Raymond, she urges us: Build yourselves a place within the cave of your heart, build a sense of God, of Jesus dwelling within you. Within the cave of her heart Catherine came to understand her own creatureliness, and a sense of her own littleness. She is nothing, God is everything. With this knowledge, she also understood she was created in love. In the very same moment that she has this sense of her own nothingness there is also the realization that she is something splendidly made, the work of God's love.

She also comes to a realisation that just as she has been created in love – she is also redeemed in love through the shedding of blood. She looks through sin to the gift of the love of God expressed in creation and redemption. We are redeemed in love. The Father assures her: "I am God love."

Growing in the Spirit of St Dominic

This knowledge of herself triggers a compassionate understanding of others, our weakness and our need. Catherine invites us to enter her own experience, to abandon being self reliant and self-sufficient. Emptiness and an awareness of our human frailty in constant need of God's love are the ground of her relationship with God. As Mary Magdalene met Jesus outside the tomb, Catherine invites us to turn inwards and meet Jesus at home in our own hearts.

Is it true that the last child tends to be spoilt? It is no surprise then, that Catherine was a bit precocious, self-willed. She knew how to stamp her foot and get what she wanted.

After a year of confrontation with the family, her father Giacomo stepped in to declare a peace. She got her way and the longed for solitude of her room. For three years Catherine lived in the seclusion of her home only going out to Mass in Santo Domingo. When she was seventeen/eighteen she applied to join the Lay Dominicans. At first the group resisted, judging Catherine too young but she got her way and joined them at prayer.

At prayer she spoke with the Lord as a friend talks to a friend. Illiterate, Catherine asked: "If it is your will that I should sing the psalms please teach me yourself". He did. She loved the phrase "O Lord, come to my aid. O Lord, make haste to help me". When it was time for a meal He told her to be off to eat. A colourful, strong, passionate and enthusiastic personality she put all of herself into whatever she did.

At the age of twenty, the Lord called Catherine to leave her solitude and to combine a life of apostolic activity with one of prayer. "Your cell will no longer be your dwelling place. For the salvation of souls, you will leave the city of your birth. I shall be with you always." She was not pleased and resisted. She feared that it would separate her from the Lord. He reassured her: "I have no intention of parting you from myself, but rather of making sure to bind you to me all the closer, by the bond of your love for your neighbour."

> "Remember that I have laid down two commandments of love: love of me and love of your neighbour... On two feet, you must walk my way. On two wings, you must fly to heaven. I shall be your guide in everything it will be your lot to do."

The same appeal he makes to us. Accompanied by Mona Lappa she began to visit the hospitals in Siena, nursing the sick. She loved the Misericordia, the house of Mercy. She, also, visited the sick in their homes. Outside the walls of the town was the leprosarium. Here Catherine looked after Tecca. Old, suffering from leprosy, Tecca had a vile tongue, Catherine visited her twice daily but every time Catherine came to visit, Tecca poured abuse upon her. Mona Lappa was

Short Lives

furious with the way she slandered Catherine and forbade Catherine to visit her. Catherine nursed her to the end and Tecca died repentant.

Quickly, Catherine's ministry grew. Asked by the city to settle disputes between different warring families she was asked to negotiate peace between the city of Florence and the Holy See. She set out for Avignon on a donkey accompanied by several of her loyal companions. She failed to negotiate a peace but met the Pope, Gregory II. She cajoled him and at last persuaded him to return to Rome. He set sail, she travelled by land and reached Genoa first. By the time his ship reached the port Gregory was filled with doubts about the wisdom of returning to Rome. Secretly, simply dressed, he visited Catherine who gave him courage to complete the journey.

He died within a year and was succeeded by Urban Vl. Urban had a difficult temperament. The Western schism fell upon the Church. Catherine wrote to him, berated him for his tactlessness and lack of mercy in dealing with people. "Justice", she wrote, "must be set in mercy." The Pope who imprisoned some of his cardinals went in awe of her: "This little woman is too much for me."

The Lord encouraged her and promised support: "Empty yourself for your neighbour but do it for him and you will be filled as you empty yourself." A group of disciples gathered round her – lay people, religious, priests, poets.

One of her most dramatic interventions concerned Niccolo di Toldo. A young man from Perugia he made some remarks about the Sienese government and was sentenced to death. Catherine describes her visit to him in prison and helped him to die with courage.

> "I went to visit him… he was consoled and made his confession… He made me promise that for the love of God I would be with him at the time of his execution. In the morning before the bell tolled I went to him… I took him to Mass and he received the Eucharist… there remained a fear that he would not be brave at the last moment…'Stay with me and do not leave me and then I cannot but be well and will die content.' 'I will wait for you at the place of execution and I think his heart lost all fear… I waited at the place of execution in continual prayer… seeing me he laughed and asked me to make the sign of the cross over him… He knelt and stretched out his neck and I bent down over him… he kept repeating 'Jesus and Catherine' and as he said the words I received his head into my hands…"

> "When… love for me and love for your neighbour – are gathered together… you find that I am your companion, and I am your strength and your security. " D. 54

Growing in the Spirit of St Dominic

Intercession

Her prayer, like Dominic's, is marked by intercession, the prayer of asking. As she was dying, she repeated Dominic's promise to the brothers. She comforted those about her: "I shall be with you always and be of more use to you in heaven than I was on earth." In other words, ask me to intercede for you.

It is her sense of being loved that empowers her to turn to God and plead for the needs of others.

> "It is I who gave you the hunger and the voice with which you call me... Never lower your voice in crying out to me to be merciful to the world." "I give to those who ask, and I invite you to ask. And I am very displeased with those who do not knock...." D. 107

Love alone is the cause of creation. We are loved into existence. It is a love for all creation, a love for Catherine and for each single person.

> "Open the eye of your understanding, then, and look at my hand, and you will see that what I have told you is true. So in obedience to the most high Father, she raised her eyes, and saw within his closed fist the entire world. And God said: My daughter, see now and know that no one can be taken from me. Everyone is here as I said, either in justice or in mercy. They are mine, I created them, and love them ineffably. And so in spite of their wickedness, I will be merciful to them because of my servants, and I will grant what you have asked of me with such love and sorrow."

Aware of this Catherine can then turn to God and plead for sinners.

> "I beg it as a favour, that you have mercy on your people with the same eternal love that leads you to create us in your image and likeness... with unimaginable love you looked upon your creatures within your very self, and you fell in love with us. So it was love that made you create us and give us being just so that we might taste your supreme eternal good... For love! You, God, became human and we have been made divine. In the name of your unspeakable love, then, I beg you, I would force you even! to have mercy on your creatures." D. 13

Catherine puts herself before God as totally poor and powerless. 'I am small' she cries before she begins to intercede for the world and the Church. And we too can say 'I am small', "totally poor and powerless. With the same conviction as Catherine, we can turn to the Lord and remind him of his words: "If in my name you ask me for anything, I will do it." Jn. 14:14

The Power of the Blood

Catherine's devotion to the Precious Blood is a key in intercession. She urges us to make our own the cry of the blood.

Short Lives

Empty yourself for your neighbour but do it for him and you will be filled as you empty yourself. L. 49

Simon Roche, OP

- "Build yourself a cell within your own heart and never put a foot outside it."

- "On two feet, you must walk my way. On two wings, you must fly to heaven. I shall be your guide in everything it will be your lot to do."

- "Empty yourself for your neighbour but do it for him and you will be filled as you empty yourself." L.49

- "When love for me and love for your neighbour are gathered together...you find that I am your companion, and I am your strength and your security." D. 54

- "It is I who gave you the hunger and the voice with which you call me... Never lower your voice in crying out to me to be merciful to the world." "I give to those who ask, and I invite you to ask. And I am very displeased with those who do not knock....D. 107
- "I am God love".

- "I shall be with you always and be of more use to you in heaven than I was on earth."

Eternal God,
Restore health to the sick,
And life to the dead.
Give us a voice to cry to you,
For mercy for the world,
And for reform of holy Church.
Listen to your own voice
With which we cry out to you.

Prayer of St Catherine

Growing in the Spirit of St Dominic

St Martin de Porres

The Baptismal register in Lima reads: *Martin, son of an unknown father.* When John de Porres saw that the colour of the baby's skin was black, he refused to recognise him as his son. Very politely, he walked away and abandoned Martin and his mother.

Martin grew up with the stigma of his birth. People taunted him. How did he feel? How would any of us feel? Humiliated? Bitter?

If Martin felt bitter, he confronted it in himself, came to terms with the hurt and abandonment of those years but it did something to him. It gave birth to a well of compassion for all those hurt in any way, those who themselves had been abandoned, the sick the lonely and especially the poor.

The Plague
Childhood is the rib cage about which the shape of life is formed. In December 1591, when Martin was twelve years old, an event occurred which was to shape his life. A ship arrived from Spain. Many had died, others were seriously ill. It carried the plague known as the Black Death, which rapidly spread throughout the city. Martin immediately offered himself as a helper in the hospital of St Lazarus. Imagine how his mother felt! He nursed the sick and dying, bathing the fevered bodies of plague victims. It was a harrowing time, fear everywhere and no known cure. Martin resolved to become a healer.

With help sent by his father he was apprenticed to Mathew Pastor a barber and surgeon. He became Martin's life long friend and his greatest benefactor. Over the next three years, he learnt to bind-up wounds, prepare medicines from herbs, set broken limbs, acquiring the medical knowledge of the time for the relief of the sick and diseased. Word of his skill quickly spread.

Present to God, Present to the World
Each day he visited the Church of St Lazarus where he served Mass and he was often seen praying before the altar of Our Lady of the Rosary in the Dominican Church. Here, he brought his problems and the growing desire to become a Dominican. At fifteen, he entered the priory and at twenty-four he was professed as a Dominican Brother. He loved the chapter room and it's Cross. Eyes fixed on the crucifix he meditated on the sufferings of Jesus. Each day he did penance for his sins, for the salvation of others, and for the souls in purgatory. He wore a rosary round his neck and every morning rose at four o'clock to greet the new day from the Church tower where he prayed to Our Lady. Regularly, he brought fresh flowers to the statue of Our Lady at the entrance to the refectory and lit a candle.

Short Lives

A man of prayer, God made Martin a neighbour to other peoples needs, their pain, poverty, bereavement, and loneliness. Daily the poor and the sick gathered at the priory in Lima. One day in 1635, Martin saw a youngster among those waiting for food, poorer and more emaciated than all the others, so sick that he could barely walk. He didn't even have a shirt to protect him from the sun. Martin asked: "Where do you come from? 'Spain', he replied. How old are you? 'Fourteen!'" At fourteen John Vasquez had crossed the Atlantic to seek his fortune and found himself on the streets of Lima with nothing to eat, no clothes, no trade and extremely ill.

Years later, John Vasquez recalled that day and how Martin had taken him to his room, nursed him back to health, clothed and fed him and later taught him a trade. John asked Martin to allow him to help him in the care of the poor and the sick. He was one of the most important witnesses at the process for Martin's canonisation. Martin overcame his own sense of unwantedness, not by going into himself and down into the well of self pity but by reaching out to others in their need.

Who were Martin's poor? The sick, the hungry, the lonely and abandoned of Lima's streets. Everyday he fed the hundred's who came to the priory and like Dominic, he gathered others round him to care for the needy. They brought him medical supplies, clothes and food and the help of their hands.

Street Children

A great concern were the abandoned children of Lima's streets. Martin pleaded on their behalf and Matthew Pastor came to his help. They opened a house and started the school of the Holy Cross.

There were regular visits to the prison. He always brought something. On one occasion he ran out of bread and pawned his hat to buy something for two prisoners. For weeks, he walked five miles to bring food to a group of starving soldiers who had not received their pay.

One day returning to the priory he found a poor Indian who had been repeatedly stabbed. Near death from loss of blood, Martin stanched the flow of the blood and carried him to the priory putting him into his own bed. It wasn't the first time! Earlier he had put an old man covered with sores into his bed and members of the community complained. He had been asked not to do it again. When confronted with the sick Indian, Martin replied: "I always thought charity was more important than obedience." He knew his theology.

Growing in the Spirit of St Dominic

The Bulls of Limitambo

Martin knew how to relax. He loved his visits to the farm called Limitambo. There were young bulls. Strong and energetic he liked nothing better than to play the toreador. Holding a piece of cloth, he would play the bulls. As they charged down on him, he nimbly stepped aside at the last moment while others laughed and enjoyed the fun from the safety of the fence.

He was a joyous man, knew how to laugh and radiate joy in others. Witness after witness at the process of canonisation spoke of his smile. He also had the extraordinary gift of being present to people at the moment of their need. Strong and fearless, he lived in the conviction of God's love and support.

Simon Roche, OP

Short Lives

Giorgio Frassati
Man of the Beatitudes

What! A university student beatified, you're joking! On May 20th 1990 John Paul II beatified twenty four year old Pier Giorgio Frassati. Pier Giorgio was born in Turin, Italy, in 1901. His father, an agnostic was the founder of the newspaper La Stampa, his mother an artist. At school with the Jesuits, he was a healthy happy young man excelling at sport.

School was followed by the study of engineering. In Italy it was a time of reconstruction after the First World War and there was little interest in religion. Pier Giorgio was remarkable, he was a daily communicant. Mischievous and a joker he was known as "Robespierre" or the "Terror" to his friends. Besides the busy life of a young university student he formed a group to discuss the faith. In 1918 he joined the Vincent de Paul and spent much of his free time helping the sick and the needy. At graduation given the choice of money or a car he chose the money and gave it to the needy. He found a room for an old woman evicted from her tenement, provided a bed for an invalid with tuberculosis and supported the three children of a sick widow.

In 1919 he joined the Catholic Student Federation and the Popular Party which promoted Catholic Teaching. His plea was: "Charity is not enough, we need social reform." In 1922 he joined the Lay Dominicans.

An enthusiastic sportsman he was at the centre of students activity, his great love was mountain climbing. While cultivating a deep inner life, Pier Giorgio was involved in Catholic action. He did not preach at people, but his unselfconscious goodness, good humour, genuine kindness and interest in others exerted a strong influence on his companions. At the Vincent de Paul he was the first to volunteer for any work, giving everything he had. Without setting out to do so, many sought him as their spiritual guide. As his university days grew to a close he expressed the desire to become a lay missionary and so use his engineering skills in the lay apostolate. He longed to get married and begin his own family and dreamt of establishing a home for the destitute and old people of Turin. It wasn't to be.

As a young man he stayed at the home of Karl Rahner. He wrote about the young Italian student who so influenced him. "Pier Giorgio, represented the pure, happy handsome youth given to prayer, enthusiastic about everything that is free and beautiful, interested in social problems, and had the Church and its fate at heart... a Christian, simply, and in an absolutely spontaneous way, as if it were something spontaneous for everybody. He had the strength and courage to be what he is... that God is, that what sustains us is prayer, that the Eucharist nourishes what is eternal in us, that all people are brothers and sisters... he

Growing in the Spirit of St Dominic

became a spontaneous Christian, a church going catholic, without therefore saying "Amen" to all ecclesiastical traditions, full of apostolic zeal, always ready to help his neighbour in a practical way. None of this is explained either by his family situation or the cultural and religious situation of the time… "Here we perceive in a mysterious way that God's grace is not something predictable. Here suddenly is again a Christian in an environment which makes us think that such a phenomenon belongs to the past… His special work, love for the poor, responsibility in facing the wretchedness of others were so genuine and so deep, so charged with the spirit of sacrifice in Pier Giorgio as to make him an exception among the many Christian young people of his time… there must have been few who while suffering the torments of death by poliomyelitis still would feel it is his duty to think of the poor."

The truth is that he was an average student. In college he constantly put off exams. His mother's letters frequently scold. Then he would spend nights studying, dazed for lack of sleep. The tune never changed. He was accused of wasting time, stubbornness, even lying without understanding what he was doing. Neither, father or mother understood their son. Unhappily married their relationship was ending.

Marianne Cerutti, a poor woman who polished the floors at La Stampa scolded his father for failing to understand him. Marianne, a socialist revolutionary knew many things about Pier Giorgio's secret life. She knew whose homes he went to, when he jokingly told her he went out to make his "conquests". She knew the network of good works that caught him in the city. Study was only part of his day and although he considered it his first duty, he often came to it only after a considerable time spent with the poor, a session in the St Vincent de Paul conference or a night spent in Adoration. Daily Mass and communion was the breath of his life. When a friend asked him why do you study engineering when you want to be a missionary he replied that without a professional preparation he could not make his apostolate effective.

Beneath the smiling exterior of the restless university student was concealed the amazing life of a committed Christian in a society which was indifferent and sometimes even hostile to the Church. John Paul II suggests that Pier Giorgio's life finds a voice in the words of St Peter: "Sanctify Christ as Lord in your heart. Always be ready to give an explanation to anyone who asks for a reason for your hope." 1.Pet. 3.:5.

My Model is Savonarola
On the 28 May 1922 in San Domenico, festively lit for the feast of St Dominic he joined the Lay Dominicans and took the name Girolamo after his personal hero, the Dominican preacher and reformer, Savonarola. To anyone who greeted him in that name he replied: "May I imitate him in the struggle and in virtue." He

Short Lives

shared his enthusiasm with a friend who wanted to follow his example. "I am so happy that you want to become part of the big family of St Dominic... This name (Girolamo) recalls a figure who is dear to me and certainly to you too, as you share my feelings against corrupt morals: the figure of Fra Girolamo Savonarola, whose name I most unworthily bear. I am a fervent admirer of that friar, who died as a saint at the stake. In becoming a Lay Dominican I wanted to take him as a model, but I am far from being like him."

Just before receiving his university degree in June 1925 Pier Giorgio developed polio. His illness coincided with that of his grandmother and went unnoticed. When diagnosed it was too late. On the eve of his death, his hand paralysed, he scribbled a note to a friend reminding him about injections for Converso a needy student, and asked his sister to care for the families he helped.

He died at the age of twenty four. His charity towards others was nourished in the Eucharist, night adoration, the Letters of St Paul, in particular his frequent meditation on the Way of Charity outlined in 1.Cor.13, and by the writings of St Catherine of Siena. He loved the Rosary and prayed it three times a day after becoming a Lay Dominican.

Marie Ronan and Simon Roche OP

"I want to be able to help my people in every way and I can do this better as a layman than as a priest, because in our country priests do not have as much contact with the people."

John Paul II, at the Beatification

"Pier Giorgio is also the man of our century, the modern man, the man who has loved much... the master to be followed... With him the Gospel turns to welcoming solidarity, intense truth seeking, as well as a demanding commitment to justice. Prayer and contemplation silence and reception of the sacraments give tone and substance to his varied apostleship and his whole life enlivened by the Spirit of God... He made a mark upon our entire century... His love for beauty and art, his passion for sports and the mountains, his attention to society's problems did not inhibit his relationship with the Absolute. Entirely immersed in the mystery of God and totally dedicated to the constant service of his neighbour."

Growing in the Spirit of St Dominic

Jonathan W. Nobles

Lay Dominicans are a mixed bag of saints and sinners. This is the story of Jonathan Nobles. On the feast of Our Lady of the Rosary, 7th of October 1998, Jonathan Nobles was executed by lethal injection at Huntsville prison, Texas. Jonathan was a Lay Dominican trying to follow Jesus in the Spirit of St Dominic.

In 1986, high on drugs Jonathan, then 25 years of age, stabbed two young women to death and seriously injured Ron Ross, a horrific crime for which he was sentenced to death. He was convicted almost entirely on the strength of his own confession. He never took the stand during his trial. He sat impassively as the guilty verdict was read out and only flinched slightly when the judge sentenced him to death. When he arrived at Ellis prison he quickly alienated himself from the guards and most of the prisoners. But somehow in what is among the most inhumane environments in the civilised world Jonathan began to change.

In Huntsville Jonathan underwent a conversion and entered the Church. A group of eleven young men present at the time of his admission to the Church were members of the St Martin de Porres Chapter. Through them he became interested in the Lay Dominicans and was received into their Chapter in 1989. In 1991 he made his final commitment and was instrumental in introducing other prisoners to the Lay Dominicans. He developed a deep devotion to the Rosary and Catherine of Siena.

For eight years Jonathan was a spiritual leader on death row breaking the Good News to those who themselves faced the same sentence. He stood as godfather at the baptism of Cliff Boggess a fellow inmate and later helped officiate at the Mass celebrated the night before Cliff Boggess was executed. He encouraged his companions to experience God's word in the scriptures, invited others to attend the celebration of the Eucharist. He loved the Eucharist and taught non-Catholics to present themselves to receive a blessing at the time of Communion.

For ten years Steve Earle, the country musician, corresponded with Jon who asked him to be a witness at his execution. Ten days before this took place Steve came to visit Jonathan. Jonathan sought forgiveness and reconciliation from those he had injured and whose lives he had taken and suffered the pain of not being able to be reconciled to all.

Three months before his death he appeared on T.V. and donated his kidneys: "I want to do something good before I die." Five days before his execution fr Chris Eggleton visited Jonathan. They prayed and talked together for several hours. Jonathan told his story and shared some of his poetry, spoke of his love of Mary, the Rosary and St Dominic, his "fire" for preaching and work for the conversion of others. Chris describes his visit:

> "Jonathan placed his hands flat up against the plexiglas divide which separated us and I placed my hands up against his... alternating we prayed."

Jonathan met Bishop Carmody when he celebrated Mass for the inmates. He asked the bishop to be one of the witnesses at his execution. "I said I would be there with him, and a promise made is a debt unpaid... I made sure I would keep my promise."

Jonathan fasted on his last day. When asked what would he like for his last meal he said he would like the Eucharist. He called it "spiritual food for the journey home".

The funeral Mass was held at St Thomas an hour after Jonathan was pronounced dead. Jonathan was laid out in the Dominican habit, bishop Carmody celebrated the Mass with others. Jonathan had chosen the readings and the hymns. A few days after his death Chris Eggleton received a letter Jonathan wrote the night before he died.

> "I pray that Our Lord bless you, and that his Spirit rest upon you; filling you with true peace and joy. I am very sorry that I do not have the ability to share in greater length with you here on earth or even in this letter. However be assured that I shall pray for you in heaven with Dominic, Mary and all of our Dominican Family."

Simon Roche, OP

Growing in the Spirit of St Dominic

Agnes McLaren
1837-1913

Duncan McLaren started work at twelve years, at twenty-four he opened his own business in Edinburgh, Scotland and through reading and attending lectures he made up for a lost education. Successful in business, he entered politics. He campaigned for the repeal of the Corn Laws, and the education of the poor. A Liberal, he championed the needs of the growing industrial classes and the needs of little people and was successful in establishing a system of free schools in Edinburgh.

Agnes was the first child of his second marriage. Duncan was always there for the family and a healer in his own way. When one of the boys began stammering and it grew worse his father called him one day. "Now lad I am going to cure you of your stammering. Open your mouth and put out your tongue." Duncan took a gold pencil from his pocket, laid it on his tongue and said: "Now go away, you will never stammer again." His stammer never returned. When asked about it, Duncan told his wife: "It is just faith."

Agnes grew up in a home schooled in social justice. A political family, Duncan and his wife encouraged discussion. Duncan was a Presbyterian, his wife a Quaker, with a long tradition of social involvement. It made for an interesting home.

As Agnes grew, she became involved in the fight for women's liberation Her sister sought to be accepted as a student of medicine in Edinburgh but was refused. Women in medicine were considered a scandal! The needs of poor women led Agnes on the same path. Impossible in Britain, she sought to be accepted as a medical student in France. She applied to the University of Montpellier and was accepted. She stayed with Franciscan Sisters, joined them for Mass each morning and in 1878 qualified in medicine in both Montpellier and Dublin. She returned to practice medicine in France and was received into the Church in November 1898.

Remembering a ruined Dominican priory in Scotland, she read about the Order and its re-establishment in France by Lacordaire. She heard of the Dominican Bethany Sisters at Montferrand founded by Pere Lataste, OP. and set out to visit them.

The inspiration for Bethany was Dominic's foundation at Toulouse for girls working the streets. Agnes felt it was the fulfilment of her dream to help women in need. She visited Rome, met the Master of the Order, fr Cormier and was received as a Lay Dominican.

Short Lives

At 68 years, life was only beginning for Agnes McLaren. Through contact with Mill Hill in London, the plight of poor women in India and the absence of women doctors became her next passion. She took inspiration from Catherine of Siena and her work at the Ospedale Grande in Genoa. Through her efforts Agnes helped to open a hospital in Rawlpindi.

Seventy years young, Agnes set sail for India and threw herself into all the problems of a mission hospital. She knocked on doors and wrote letters for help. The great need was to have sisters trained as doctors and surgeons to meet the needs of women.

Canon Law needed to be changed! Like Dominic, Agnes besieged churchmen and the Holy See. She made six visits to Rome passionately urging change, refusing to take no for an answer.

In 1912, conscious of her age and growing ill health Agnes felt that her days were numbered and the hope of her heart, the establishment of medical missions for women remained unfulfilled. Providence led her to Anna Dengel to whom she communicated her inspiration. The future foundress of the Medical Missionary Sisters would fulfil Agnes dream. Agnes died in 1913, her hearts desire safe in another's hands.

Simon Roche, OP

Growing in the Spirit of St Dominic

Honoria Magaen and Honoria Burke

It is a far cry from the priory of Burrishoole two miles west of Newport, Co. Mayo to the Dominican priory in Taromina in Sicily. During a chance visit to the priory in 1921 Msg. Cullen of the Dublin Archdiocese discovered the connection. In the cloister of the priory, now a hotel, he found a fresco which depicts a woman standing in the hollow of a tree with the title Bl Honoria Magaen, D'Ibernia. Blessed Honorio Magaen of Ireland. The artist is unknown. The fresco was painted shortly after 1656.

Who was Honoria Magaen, what is her story? Felix O'Connor writing on the 17th of May 1653 records it for us. He was the prior in Kilkenny when the city surrendered to Cromwell in March 1650. Excluded from the pardon granted by Cromwell, Felix escaped and made his way to Connacht and the Dominican priory at Burrishoole. He was elected prior. "Here for three years I was constantly giving shelter to other religious who were refugees. At length the heretics arrived on the scene. They attacked but were twice driven back. A furious third assault succeeded and they burst into the building. They killed all the soldiers I had with me. Some of the brothers were wounded, some taken prisoners while others escaped to the mountains. I myself, with a boy managed to get out a canoe and in that tiny boat launched out into the deep… in that little canoe made out of a single tree trunk we made it to Clare Island in safety."

It wasn't long before the Cromwellians arrived. The island was surrounded by seven ships and twenty two small boats. The sentence of those who had taken refuge there was exile, death if they returned. Felix O'Connor must have reached Clare Island sometime before the 20th of October and the attack on the Dominican priory at Burrishoole about the 15th February.

Honoria de Burgo and Honoria Magaen were Lay Dominicans living in a house close to the priory at Burrishoole. They died in February 1653. Before the February attack on the priory they escaped to Saints Island about a mile away in Loch Furness. Soldiers pursued them to the island and caught them. They stripped them of their clothes. Honoria Burke was 104 years and was thrown into the boat, her ribs broken and she died almost immediately. Honoria Magaen was mercilessly beaten but as the boat neared the shore she escaped into the surrounding woods and took refuge in the hollow trunk of a tree. The girl who had accompanied them to the island carried Honoria Burke on her shoulders back to the Dominican Church and placed her before the altar of Our Lady. Next morning Honoria Magaen was found in the hollow of the tree frozen to death.

Their story fired the imagination of an unknown Italian artist who recalled their heroism in the cloister fresco in Taromina. But for his brush, their story would be forgotten.

Short Lives

Their inspiration was St Catherine of Sienna. From the parish of Burrishoole and visiting the priory, Honoria Burke heard the story of Catherine. Inspired, she set her heart on following St Dominic in the spirit St Catherine.

Honoria was born about 1549. At the age of fourteen she was received as a Lay Dominican by Thaddeus O'Duane the provincial. She and her companions lived in a house close to the priory. Here they spent their lives in prayer and ministering to the needs of the people. Stories survive of the flour bin which was so often emptied to help the hungry and was mysteriously replenished, and the unknown youth who knocked on their door with provisions during a time of great need.

In 1580 a band of soldiers descended on Burrishoole and fearing the worst Honoria and her companions fled to the mountains returning after they departed. Remote, it may have been, but eventually the Cromwellian forces descended on Burrishoole Priory and the sisters house. The Acts of Dominican Chapter of 1656 give an account of the death of Honoria Burke and Honoria Magaen:

> "In her fourteenth year Honoria Burke took the habit of the third Order, that is of St Catherine of Sienna, at the hands of Thaddeus O'Duane, the Irish Provincial. She erected a house near the church of our priory of Burrishoole... she led a very holy life... In the last persecution of Cromwell, with another of her community Honoria Magaen and a maid, she fled to saints Island. They were pursued by their persecutors, seized, stripped of their clothes, though it was the month of February and mid-winter. After breaking three of her ribs, these cruel men flung her into a boat, as if she were a bundle of sticks, and let her die. She was taken by her servant on her shoulders to the church of Burrishoole; there she was laid before the altar of the Blessed Virgin. The servant left her for a little while to go in search of the other sister in the wood. On her return she found Honoria kneeling before the altar, with head erect as if in prayer, sleeping calmly in the Lord."

> "Honoria Magaen... would not be separated in death from her whose labours and hardships she had shared in life. She was stripped of her clothing and wounded... she escaped from the hands of these madmen, fled into a neighbouring wood and concealed herself in the hollow of a tree. The next day she was found there frozen to death. Both were buried in the same tomb."

Simon Roche OP

A Journey in the Spirit
A brief account of the spiritual journey of Aidan O'Neill, a Lay Dominican in Belfast.

Early Years
The story of my spiritual journey begins on the 13th June 1977, the night of my mother's death. I was born before the Second World War into a happy family in Omagh. The only shadow was a severe and ongoing problem with my eyes. I remember two Christmases having bandages removed from my eyes to see my presents. Then the bandages were put on again.

When I went to school, I lost a lot of time because I had one eye or the other bandaged. I remember that when I got home from school, the first thing to do was to sit down and bathe my eyes with warm water, and what my mother called, "Borassic Powder." This continued all through primary. I also remember being in the County Hospital in Omagh on a number of occasions.

When I was twelve I was taken to the Eye & Ear Hospital in Derry, under Dr Killen and was there for four of five weeks. My mother visited me regularly. On one occasion, she went away saying she would be back later. She didn't come and I went to sleep, only to be wakened by my mother, who told me to get dressed, she was taking me home. I remember the nurses were angry, but I wasn't told why. I was sent back to school, and never had any more problems with my eyes. Soon, I had forgotten all about them. It was 1945. I didn't get an explanation until the night before my mother died.

Events surrounding my Mothers Death
In June 1977, we knew mother was dying. For six years she didn't seem to know anyone. As I had to return to Belfast, I volunteered to keep vigil on the Sunday night. I had just turned away from the bed, when suddenly she spoke. I got an awful shock. I looked back at her, and her eyes were wide open, very bright and clear. Then, began a dialogue that went on through the night, an awful lot of it was eye contact, but at times she spoke very clearly. She told me things about myself that I had never heard. At one point, she said, "Your eyes are very precious, look after them." It was then that she told me about the day in 1945 when she had brought me home from the hospital in Derry. Dr Killen had sent for her and explained that my right eye was beyond repair and asked permission to remove it. She asked him whether this would mean that the left eye would be alright and he said that he could guarantee nothing. "But what is certain, is that if the right eye is not removed, Aidan will be blind in both eyes in a matter of months." She asked for time to think about it and went to St Eugene's Cathedral. She prayed for hours, and finally made a promise to say three Rosaries every day until the day she died if my eyes were spared. She then got the strength to come

A Journey in the Spirit

back to the hospital, and insisted on bringing me home, despite the protests of the nurses. She kept her promise, because after the Family Rosary, she would go on to say two more Rosaries by herself. We never knew the reason.

Several times during the night, I could see her getting fretful. She would ask, "Get Emily for me." Emily Polly had been a fellow patient with my mother, and they had shared a room and become very close friends. Emily was Church of Ireland. She took increasing care of mother as she deteriorated.

Look after your back
Mother also brought up the subject of my back: "Look after your back." This was a reference to an incident in my youth. When I returned to school after the cure of my eyes I began to take an interest in sports, particularly athletics. In 1950, I was picked for the Irish Catholic Students' Olympic team in four events. I got to the final in all and took second place in the javelin. Fairly soon after that, I had an awful accident. The physical training instructor coaxed me into doing an exercise I had never tried before, a backward flip while lying prone on my back. As a result I sustained a back injury and suffered intensely for three years. My mother heard about a priest in the Passionist monastery at The Graan, Enniskillen, called Fr Leo, who was reputed to have healing powers. We drove down to see him in my brother Pat's car, only to be told he was away on retreat. Another young priest prayed with me, and told us, "Say the family Rosary for three nights, and he'll be all right if it is God's will."

On the way home, there was excruciating pain worse than anything I had experienced before. They managed to get me up to bed, and as I lay there in agony a thought came into my mind that the young priest had said: "Say the Rosary." So, I forced myself out of bed, into a kneeling position, and started saying the Rosary. No sooner had I started, than I realized my back was cured, and I was able to move freely. This great healing was of course remembered in our family, and this was what my mother referred to on the night she was dying.

It was a night of wonderful love. I remember my mother saying to me, "I have nothing to give you but my faith." I asked: "Mummy, would you like me to say a Rosary for all the Rosaries you said for me?" She nodded, so I started to say the Rosary for both of us. Just as I was giving out the title of the fifth glorious mystery, the Crowning of Our Lady as Queen of Heaven, I had to stop. I was amazed, my mother's face had suddenly changed, and instead of the wrinkled old face of an eighty five year old, I was looking at the face of a young girl. After I had taken it in, I said to her: "Mummy, do you know your face is completely changed? You have the face of a young girl." I put my hands on either side of her face, and the feel of the skin was that of a young person. I then continued with the fifth decade, full of amazement. I think her face remained like that until the end of the decade, and then returned to its normal state.

Soon after my sister Chris arrived. Immediately, I said to her, "Come on, we've got to go and get Emily. Mummy wants to see her before she dies." We arrived at the Nursing Home about 8.00 am. The matron said, "I couldn't let Emily go to a death bed, she is subject to epilepsy." I walked round her desk sat on her chair, and said: "Look, I'm not leaving without Emily." She suggested that we go down to Emily's room. Emily was sitting on the end of her bed, fully clothed, with her hat and coat on and handbag on the bed beside her. The matron asked, "Emily, what are you doing up and dressed at this hour of the morning?" "Oh, matron," she replied, "Mrs O'Neill has been crying for me all night, and I have to go up and see her." The Matron gave in, and we took Emily to the Hospital. When we arrived in my mother's room, she almost climbed into the bed, so eager was she to put her arms around her and comfort her. There was a period of loving communication between them, and shortly afterwards, mother died peacefully.

Urgent business required my presence in Belfast at the earliest possible moment, so after I had a couple of hours' sleep in my sister's house, I set off by car. On the way, I was so full of celebration and joy at what had happened that I started singing hymns. Before long, I was singing in a different way, babbling like a child. It somehow seemed to me that this expressed the joy and thanksgiving of the hymns, only better. I had never heard of the charismatic movement, or of "singing in tongues". This went on, all the way back to Belfast. A friend of mine later rang the house to reassure herself. She had seen me travelling in the opposite direction, and thought it strange that I appeared to be laughing and singing. Perhaps, she thought I was drunk!

My life is changed
The days of my mother's death and its aftermath saw a big change in my life. I was born again, on 7th June, 1977. Initially, I contented myself by saying three Rosaries every day, as my mother had done, and this went on for a few years. I knew that I would be called to do something more, but waited for the Lord to show me. Then Fr Doherty told me that he had started Marriage Encounter at St Clement's, and soon he had me deeply involved. That took my spiritual energy but didn't fully satisfy.

A great blessing was given to me. A man called Billy Mitchell, along with two neighbours Lois and Angus McPherson, started an inter-faith Bible Study Group. Twelve to fourteen of us started meeting in one another's houses. Noreen and I noticed how our Protestant neighbours were able to quote chapter and verse, they had a deep love of the Bible. We were shocked by our ignorance.

A Journey in the Spirit

I didn't even know my way round the Bible. I started first on the New Testament, and as a hunger for Scripture grew went on to the Old. Before long, reading the Bible was taking up most of my spare time.

Shortly afterwards I went to Lourdes. Some of the helpers were girls in the Charismatic Renewal movement. I was interested enough to enquire where they met, and so headed off one evening for Shirley Hall in Belfast with some trepidation. The sight of what appeared to me to be a tall, slim balding Protestant Minister taking the meeting almost caused me to turn on my heel, but something made me stay. The "minister" turned out to be an outstanding Catholic layman, Larry Kelly, who had introduced the Renewal in the Down & Connor diocese. I very much enjoyed that evening.

I knew immediately that God had called me to this way of prayer and I became a regular at the Shirley Hall meetings. I have been a Charismatic ever since. The Renewal is now the most important thing in my life, though I am also interested in other forms of prayer including Christian Meditation. I was baptized in the Spirit and under Larry Kelly's influence I began to spend an hour praying at lunch time.

The Lamb of God Community
During the years that followed, the Lamb of God Community has played an enormous part in my life. I was privileged to be in at the beginning. Larry said he was thinking of starting a community to deepen our commitment and we started looking for premises. A large terrace house was on the market and we all prayed for guidance. It was confirmed that we should go ahead, and we bought it, with the help of a loan from a sympathetic bank manager!

We prayed for guidance as to what we should do there. The unexpected answer was that we should open a Ladies' Hairdressing Salon on the ground floor. The house was situated in one of the very worst "inter-face" areas in North Belfast, and it was felt that it was mainly the women, from both sides of the community, who were suffering the effects of the deprivation and massive tension in the neighbourhood, particularly the women from "Tiger's Bay" (Protestant) and "New Lodge" (Catholic). The one thing we could do for them that would certainly cheer them up was provide them with inexpensive hairdos! Larry resigned from his job in Customs & Excise to devote himself full time to the Community. Members made what monetary contributions they could, and I managed to persuade the owner of the company of which I was the managing director to make an annual payment of £3,000 until the Community became self-sufficient. Somehow, we managed. These were great days for all of us, and the Lord repaid us many times over. We were full of life and exuberance using the talents God gave us. I myself felt drawn more and more to the prayer room.

Growing in the Spirit of St Dominic

The first experience I had of praying with someone was with a young lad named John from the New Lodge. John was suffering from severe eye trouble and his mother was distraught because the hospital wanted to admit him for tests. Remembering my own experiences as a child, I was deeply moved, and we prayed together and I made the Sign of the Cross over his eyes. His mother returned about ten days later. She had taken him back to the hospital. After the doctor had examined his eyes, he asked her what she had done to the boy's eyes since the last visit. He told her: "There's nothing wrong with this child's eyes." I also remember her saying, "He's a good lad, and he always says the Rosary with me", and I said to him, "Thank God that your eyes are all right, and keep saying the Rosary." There were many healings.

Jacob's Story
In the last couple of years, we had a miraculous healing within my family. In September 1999, Michelle, my son Donal's wife, found that she was pregnant. However there were complications, and she was called for a full examination, including a scan. The top gynaecologist in the Royal Victoria Hospital gave them the news that there was no fluid in her womb, and that the baby couldn't live. We decided not to tell anyone, except my son Paul, who is very ill with multiple sclerosis, and a patient in the same hospital. Somehow I had a feeling that Paul, in the extremity of his suffering, should be told, and that his prayers would be very powerful.

Another scan, brought them the news that there was now fluid in the womb, but the damage had been done, the infant's head was now too large for its body. Again, this was reported to Paul. The next month after another scan, the news was even worse, the infant's legs were not developing. The consultant could not see any hope. Michelle came over in tears.

The bad news continued with the next scan. The baby's heart was too large, and the lungs could not develop. Again, this was reported to Paul, lying in hospital, and he continued to pray. The baby was due in June 2000, but in April, Michelle developed toxaemia. She was taken into hospital for a Caesarean operation, which took place on 26th April. The consultant told Michelle that it was unlikely that the baby would be delivered alive. If alive, it would probably die very soon afterwards. Immediately the baby was born, Michelle heard it cry, and her first thought was, "How can it cry if its lungs haven't developed?" To everyone's amazement, the baby was perfectly normal in every way. Donal, who has always been of a scientific cast of mind, refusing to believe what cannot be demonstrated to him, later said to me, "I'll have to re-think everything. It's amazing. We'll have to call him Jacob. Didn't he have to fight with God to be born?" When I gave the news to Paul, tears trickled down his face. I shall always

A Journey in the Spirit

believe that it was through the prayers of Paul, in the midst of his own suffering, that this miracle happened.

April 13th 1994
On April 13th, 1994 (it is amazing to me how many important things have happened to me on the thirteenth of the month - is it something to do with Our Lady of Fatima?), my son Paul and I were shot by an unknown gunman. I had been to 5.00 p.m. Mass in the local Convent, and had gone down to the Wednesday night meeting in The Lamb of' God Community. I returned about 11.00 p.m. Noreen went to bed, and I brought Paul a hot drink, after which I was going to put him to bed. He was holding the glass in his right hand, with his left hand, which had little or no strength. I had opened the breviary, which we were going to say together, and had placed it on the arm of Paul's chair, when some thing hit me a violent blow in the chest. I was thrown back into the chair, and was aware at the same time that the glass that Paul was holding was shattered. Then I saw Paul jerk and put up his left hand to his face, shouting out at the same time, "Oh, No!" I saw the blood come spurting between his fingers. I looked down at my chest, and saw a hole in it, but slightly to the right hand side, out of which blood was spreading. Only then did I hear the shots, and I became aware of a rain of bullets coming into the room. I got up and made for the door with some vague notion of getting to the gunman, and stopping him firing at Paul. I managed to get out the front door, but there was no-one there, the firing had stopped. I remember shouting, "Police! Help! Ambulance!" Then Noreen and the two girls arrived on the scene.

Noreen got on the phone, Paul was bleeding profusely. He had four bullet wounds - two in his right shoulder, one on his right wrist (the bullet had hit his watch); while the fourth, had gone through his head, and lodged just above his left ear. I didn't think I was badly injured, I agreed however to go in the ambulance to the Mater Hospital, and it was only when the ambulance was nearly there that I found I could hardly breathe, and felt I was drowning. I later found out that the bullet had gone right through my right lung, which had filled up with blood, so that the left lung too began to fill up and hence my inability to breathe. Without treatment, I would have drowned in my own blood.

At that point, I realized, I could be dying, and remember saying, "Lord, I'm in your hands, and know you will do what is best for me. May your will be done." Immediately, I got a wonderful sense of calm. Next, I found myself saying, "Lord, please forgive the people who did this." At the hospital, I learned that Paul was to be transferred to the Neurological Unit of the Royal Victoria Hospital because of the bullet lodged in his head. We said goodbye to each other, not sure of how ill we both were, but in good spirits. Paul was operated on immediately, and thank God, the surgeons were able to extract the bullet, and he eventually made a complete recovery. The consultant ordered my transfer to the Intensive Care Unit. Later, Mr Wilson told me that the highest chance he gave either surviving the night was one in forty. He located the bullet, and could not believe it had gone through my right lung without fatally damaging any vital organ. It is still lodged in my back, too dangerous to remove. The treatment I received in the I.C.U. was superb, and I made an event free recovery being discharged after ten days. Noreen and I went down to Drumalis for ten days of prayer and rest, and my strength gradually returned and I was able to go on holidays with the family to Spain in July. When I returned in August, there was a letter waiting asking me to report to the Mater hospital. A young lady doctor told me that I had an aneurism on the aorta the main artery leading from the heart, and that I required an operation. Subsequently, I learnt that one of my kidneys was badly infected and had to be removed. Then they discovered that I needed a prostate operation. None of this would have been discovered if I had not been shot that evening in October 1994.

Aidan O'Neill

Prayers and Blessings

The Memorare
Remember O most Gracious Virgin Mary that never was it known, that anyone who fled to your protection, implored your help, or sought your intercession, was left unaided. Inspired with this confidence I turn to you Virgin of virgins my mother. To you I come before you I stand, sinful and sorrowful. O mother of the Word incarnate despise not my petitions, but in your mercy hear and answer me. Amen

St Bernard

D'Ainm Íosa
Go raibh anim milis Íosa,
Go taitneamhach scríofa ar lár mo chroíse.
A Mhuire, is a Mháthair Íosa,
Go raibh Íosa agamsa agus mise ag Íosa,
Ceangal grá a 'bheith eadrainn go brách, gan scaoileadh.
Amen, a Íosa, go brách is choíche,

Prayers of Dominican Saints

St Dominic
Lord, have mercy on your people, what will become of sinners?

Thomas Aquinas
Give us, Lord, a steadfast heart, which no unworthy affection may drag downwards; give us an unconquered heart which no sorrow may wear out; give us an upright heart which no unworthy motive may tempt aside. Bestow upon us also, Lord our God, understanding to know you, diligence to seek you, wisdom to find you, and a faithfulness that may embrace you. Amen.

For my own part,
I know,
that the chief duty
of my life
is that all that I say
and all that I feel
speaks of God.

Thomas Aquinas

Growing in the Spirit of St Dominic

Albert the Great

Lord, for the reward of eternal life, you hired me early in the morning, to work in your vineyard. Teach me Lord to fix the roots of my tree in heaven and not in the earth, that I may be found faithful, not by the foliage of words but by the fruits of good works. Grant Lord that I may be a temple of preaching; a house of prayer and of your praise for ever. Amen

Lord Jesus Christ, the great Householder, who from the first light of dawn has called me into the vineyard, when you hired me from my youth to labour in religion for the denarius of eternal life. When in judgement, evening is come and you give to the workmen their reward, what will you give to me who have stood the whole day of my life idle - not merely in the market place of the world but in the very vineyard, of religion? O Lord you do not measure our works by their public value but their internal merit before you, make me at least in the eleventh hour, change my ways that, since you are good, I may be found not entirely wanting. Amen

Catherine of Siena

Eternal God,
Restore health to the sick,
And life to the dead.
Give us a voice to cry to you,
For mercy for the world,
And for reform of holy Church.
Listen to your own voice
With which we cry out to you.
Amen

Pius V

Lord Jesus Christ,
Crucified Son of the Blessed Virgin Mary;
- Open your ears and listen to my prayers as you listened to those of the repentant thief on the Cross.
- Open your eyes and look upon me as you looked upon your dear mother from the Cross.
- Open your arms and embrace me as you embraced the whole human race with arms extended on the Cross.
- Open your heart and receive my heart, and hear me in all that I ask of you if it is agreeable to your will.

Noonday Prayer, for Lone Lay Dominicans

Dear Lord, as we pray together today, let us feel round us and in us the depth of your love and know that we are not alone. Bless our friendships with harmony and peace and help us to think of those less fortunate than ourselves. Humbly,

Prayers

we ask your forgiveness, ever remembering the way you taught us and showed us how to forgive each other. Let us praise you in all that is beautiful and true, and learn to bear with what is ugly and unfriendly. Give us your strength in hardship, and in our weakness let us find understanding and sympathy for others. Let us see in your life on Earth a gentle, ever-present light, guiding us, and in your death on the Cross, the supreme act of Love, opening the way for us to Eternal life. Let us thank you for life itself, and trust that the loving hands that made us will receive us when we die. Till the last, dear Lord, let us love and search for and pass on your Truth. Amen.

This prayer by Sylvia Spice is said by a number of lone Lay Dominicans at twelve o'clock each day in union with other Lay Dominicans.

Prayer to St Dominic for Vocations

Joyful friar, Tolerant master, Grace filled preacher, Gospel man of prayer, Pray that your sons and daughters may be faithful to your heritage of common life, common prayer, study and service. So that other men and women will join them to praise to bless and to preach that Jesus Christ is Lord. Amen.

A Dream

I dare to dream – to be as Dominic was
An ardent fiery Apostle.
A beloved and a lover fast-knit to Christ,
Radiant with his joy.

A preacher whose silent voice resounds
throughout the universe,
By love, by prayer, by quiet pondering of the
Word of life.

A compassionate listener, pleading, interceding
For mercy on the broken and needy people
of our world.

A sinner in need of redemption
identifying with my fettered brothers and sisters
who challenge me to inner freedom.

Yes, I dare to dream – to be as Dominic was
an ardent fiery Apostle
Of the glad tidings of salvation.

Siena Monastery

Growing in the Spirit of St Dominic

Lord help me,
like St Dominic
to search for the light
of truth each day.
May I live my life
as you would have me do,
and help me make this world
a place where peace and love
are stronger than
violence and disrespect. Amen

Dominican Blessing
May God the Father Bless us
May God the Son, Heal us
May the Holy Spirit Enlighten us
and give us eyes to see with
ears to hear with
hands to do the work of God with
feet to walk with
and a mouth to preach the word of salvation with,
And the angel of peace to watch over us and lead us at last,
by our Lord's gift, to the kingdom. Amen

A Selection of Prayers

Prayers for those who Mourn

We seem to give them back to you O God
Who gave them to us.
Yet, as you did not lose them in giving
So we do not lose them by their return.
Not as the world gives do you give Lover of souls.
What you give, you take not away
For what is yours is ours also, if we are yours.
And life is eternal and love is immortal,
And death is only an horizon,
And an horizon is nothing, save the limit of our sight.
Lift us up, strong Son of God, that we may see further;
Cleanse our eyes that we may see more clearly
Draw us closer to yourself
So that we may know ourselves
to be nearer to our loved ones who are with you.

Prayers

And while you prepare a place for us
Prepare us also for that happy place
That where you are
We may also be for evermore.

Bede Jarrett, OP

Old Irish Prayer
Grieve not
Nor think of me with tears,
But laugh and talk of me,
As though I were beside you.
I loved you so.
It was heaven here with you.

From a Jewish Prayer - the Kaddish
I will miss you,
and I will always yearn for you
but in submission and humility
with love and blessing, I release you
and give you back to God,
I assure myself and you
that there is nothing to fear.
Your precious soul will be safe
and well in God's holy presence,
for with God all is good.
And in case you or I have any doubts,
I proclaim and affirm
for you and for me
to hear the ancient truth:
Magnified and sanctified is the great name
of God.

Stay with us, Lord Jesus,
as evening falls:
Be our companion on our way.
In your mercy inflame our hearts
and raise our hope,
so that in union with our sisters and brothers,
we may recognise you in the scriptures
and in the breaking of bread.
May he support us all the day long,
Till the shades lengthen and the evening comes,
And the busy world is hushed

Growing in the Spirit of St Dominic

And the fever of life over
And our work is done.
Then, in his mercy,
May he give us a safe lodging
And a holy rest and peace at the last.

John Henry Newman

Help me to spread your fragrance everywhere I go
Let me preach you without preaching,
Not by words but by example,
By the catching force,
The sympathetic influence of what I do,
The evident fullness of my heart bears to you.

John Henry Newman

Breton Fisherman's Prayer
Dear God, be good to me.
The sea is so wide,
And my boat is so small.

Christ's Body
Christ has no body but yours;
Yours are the only hands with which he can do his work,
Yours are the only feet with which he can go about the world.
Christ has no body now on earth but yours.

Teresa of Avila

The Potter
It is not you who shape God.
It is God who shapes you.

If then you are the work of God, await the
hand of the artist who does all things in
due season.

Offer the potter your heart, soft and
tractable and keep the form in which the
artist has fashioned you.

Let your clay be moist lest you grow
hard and lose that imprint of the Potter's fingers.

St. Irenaeus

Prayers

Hinder not Music
Hinder not music! All your life
Is the concert of Christ your king.
And some must sing, and others must play,
And some of the music stands out always.
What matter? If only his listening ear
Is filled with the music he loves to hear,
Seek we no other thing.

And be you violin, cymbal or flute,
In this orchestra of your Lord,
Or only the drum, neither tuneful nor sweet
Yet filling all gaps with its generous beat,
Told to sing low, or told to sing high,
What matter? So long as up to the sky
Rings a full and perfect chord

Hinder not music! Keep together
With your eyes on the self-same score;
Never seeking to lead the band,
Following till the conductor's hand;
Sing in harmony, sing in measure
Sing but for this – to fill with pleasure
The heart you love and adore.

Alexis Kiely, OP

A Short Bibliography

Bedouelle, G.	St Dominic, the Grace of the World
Drane, A. T.	The Life of St Dominic
Koudelka, V. and Tugwell, S.	St Dominic
Lehner, F.C. Ed.	St Dominic, Biographical Documents (On internet)
Tugwell, S.	Saint Dominic and the Order of Preachers
Vicaire, M-H.	St Dominic and His Times
Vicaire, M-H.	The Genius of St Dominic

Aniceto Fernandez, Vincent de Couesnongle, Damian Byrne, Timothy Radcliffe,	To Praise, To Bless, To Preach
Ashley, B.	The Dominicans (On internet)
Borgman, E.	Dominican Spirituality
Jordan of Saxony,	On the Beginnings of the Order of Preachers
Murray, P.	Preachers at Prayer
Murray, P.	The New Wine of Dominican Spirituality
O'Donovan, R.	Lay Dominicans, the Way Forward
O'Donovan, R.	On Being a Lay Dominican
Tugwell, S.	Early Dominicans
Tugwell, S.	The Way of the Preacher

O'Driscoll, M.	Catherine of Siena Selected Writings
Noffke, S. trans.	Catherine of Siena: The Dialogue
Vinje, P.M.	Praying with Catherine of Siena

Faith Formation

Aquinas Thomas,	Summa Theologica (On internet)
Pinckaers Servais,	Morality: The Catholic View,
	Catechism of the Catholic Church (On internet)
Walsh, Michael,	Roman Catholicism: The Basics,
Redford, John, Ed.	Faith Alive,
Strange, Roderick,	The Catholic Faith, Oxford University Press.
Trigilio, John,	Roman Catholicism for Dummies

Lay Dominican Resources on the Internet

	Dominican Order: www.op.org/op
Within the site:	Access Laity
	Access Documents
	Rule of the Lay Fraternities
	Damian Byrne, The Laity and the Dominican Order
	Timothy Radcliffe, To Praise, To Bless, To Preach
	Other articles in section on the Laity
	Irish Province: www.dominicans.ie
Within the site:	Access Laity
Google Request	Lay Dominican Library
	Dominican Spirituality
	Dominican Documents
	Nine Ways of Prayer of St Dominic
	Dominican Saints: by name
	St Dominic: Biographical Documents
Access:	Tradition Index (A large cache of Dominican material)
Today's Good News	www.goodnews.ie

- Gospel Commentary - *For each day*
- Between Ourselves - *Our question and answer desk*
- Jacob's Well - *A different topic each month*
- Wisdom Line - *A short passage from a Spiritual Classic*
- Jesus - *Unfolding the story of Jesus*

The Priory Institute: Distance Education

In association with The University of Wales, Lampeter, the Priory Institute offers a certificate, diploma, and degree in theology. The full programme consists of twenty modules offered over five years, and while it is designed on the basis of studying two modules concurrently, participants may choose to take one module at a time. The modules are text-based, and participants receive the full text at the launch of each module, which normally takes place in The Priory Institute, Tallaght.

Email:enquiries@prioryinstitute.com
Website: www.prioryinstitute.com

Growing in the Spirit of St Dominic